BRAIN GAMES™

Consultant: Elkhonon Goldberg, Ph.D.

Publications International, Ltd

W9-DJF-444

Elkhonon Goldberg, Ph.D., ABPP/ABCN, (consultant) is a clinical professor of neurology at New York University School of Medicine, a diplomate of the American Board of Professional Psychology/American Board of Clinical Neuropsychology, and director of The East-West Science and Education Foundation. Dr. Goldberg created the Manhattan-based Cognitive Enhancement Program, a fitness center for the brain, and he is author of the internationally best-selling books *The Wisdom Paradox: How Your Mind Can Grow as Your Brain Grows Older* and *The Executive Brain: Frontal Lobes and the Civilized Mind.*

Contributing Language Consultant: Luke Haward
Contributing Writers: Elkhonon Goldberg, Ph.D.; Holli Fort
Puzzlers: Michael Adams; Cihan Altay; Myles Callum; Kelly Clark; Andrew Clarke; Jeanette Dall; Mark Danna; Harvey Estes; Josie Faulkner; Connie Formby; Peter Grabarchuk; Serhiy Grabarchuk; Dick Hess; Marilynn Huret; David Millar; Alan Olschwang; Ellen F. Pill, Ph.D.; Paul Seaburn; Fraser Simpson; Terry Stickels; Howard Tomlinson; Linda Washington
Additional Puzzle Editing: Fraser Simpson
Illustrators: Brian Babiarz, Connie Formby, Nicole H. Lee, Anna Lender, Art Mawhinney, Dave Roberts, Marilyn Roberts, Shavan R. Spears

Brain Games is a trademark of Publications International, Ltd.

Copyright © 2008 Publications International, Ltd. All rights reserved. This book may not be reproduced or quoted in whole or in part by any means whatsoever without written permission from:

Louis Weber, CEO
Publications International, Ltd.
7373 North Cicero Avenue
Lincolnwood, Illinois 60712

Ground Floor, 59 Gloucester Place
London U1U 8JJ

Permission is never granted for commercial purposes.

ISBN-13: 978-1-4127-9653-8
ISBN-10: 1-4127-9653-9

Manufactured in China.

8 7 6 5 4 3 2 1

CONTENTS

Brain Fitness   4

Assess Your Brain: Questionnaire #1   9

LEVEL 1 Turning on Your Engine   11

Get out your pencil, and start your brain working on these fun, easy puzzles.

LEVEL 2 Revving Your Motor   35

Move on to a greater challenge now that you're in gear.

LEVEL 3 Accelerate for Power   63

Feel your mental power expand as you build steam with these engaging puzzles.

LEVEL 4 Full Speed Ahead   100

Gain more mental ground as you maneuver through these difficult puzzles.

LEVEL 5 Firing on All Cylinders   137

Put the pedal to the metal to solve the most challenging puzzles of all.

Reassess Your Brain: Questionnaire #2   168

Answers   170

Index   191

BRAIN FITNESS

Your mind is your most important asset—more important than your house, your bank account, and your stock portfolio. You insure your house and work hard to pad your bank account. But what can you do to sharpen your mind and protect it from decline? With the baby boomers getting on in years, an increasing number of people are asking this question. Modern-day science provides a clear answer: You can safeguard your mind by protecting your brain. To understand this relationship further, we turn to cutting-edge research.

Protect and Enhance Your Brainpower

Modern-day neuroscience has established that our brain is a far more plastic organ than was previously thought. In the past it was believed that an adult brain can only lose nerve cells (neurons) and cannot acquire new ones. Today we know that new neurons—and new connections between neurons—continue to develop throughout our lives, even well into advanced age. This process is called *neuroplasticity*. Thanks to recent scientific discoveries, we also know that we can harness the powers of neuroplasticity in protecting and even enhancing our minds at every stage of life—including our advanced years.

How can we harness neuroplasticity to help protect and enhance our mental powers? Recent scientific research demonstrates that the brain responds to mental stimulation much like muscles respond to physical exercise. In other words, you

have to give your brain regular workouts. The more vigorous and diverse your mental life—and the more you welcome mental challenges—the more you will stimulate the growth of new neurons and new connections between them. Furthermore, the *nature* of your mental activities influences *where* in the brain this growth takes place. The brain is a very complex organ with different parts in charge of different mental functions. Thus, different cognitive challenges exercise different components of the brain.

How do we know this? We've learned this by combining experiments created from real-life circumstances with *neuroimaging*, the high-resolution technologies that allow scientists to study brain structure and function with amazing precision. Some say that these technologies have done for our understanding of the brain what the invention of the telescope has done for our understanding of the planetary systems. Thanks to these technologies, particularly MRI (magnetic resonance imaging), we know that certain parts of the brain exhibit an increased size in those who use these parts of the brain more than most people. For example, researchers found that the hippocampus, the part of the brain critical for spatial memory, was larger than usual in London cab drivers, who have to navigate and remember complex routes in a huge city. Studies revealed that the so-called Heschl's gyrus, a part of the temporal lobe of the brain involved in processing music, is larger in professional musicians than in musically untrained people. And the angular gyrus, the part of the brain involved in language, proved to be larger in bilingual individuals than in those who speak only one language.

What is particularly important is that the size of the effect—the extent to which a specific area of the brain was

enlarged—was directly related to the *amount of time* each person spent on activities that rely on that brain area. For instance, the hippocampal size was directly related to the number of years the cab driver spent on the job, and the size of Heschl's gyrus was associated with the amount of time a musician devoted to practising a musical instrument. This shows that cognitive activity directly influences the structures of the brain by stimulating the effects of neuroplasticity in these structures, since the enlargement of brain regions implies a greater-than-usual number of cells or connections between them. The impact of cognitive activity on the brain can be great enough to result in an actual increase in its size! Indeed, different parts of the brain benefit directly from certain activities, and the effect can be quite specific.

Diversify Your Mental Workout

It is also true that any relatively complex cognitive function—be it memory, attention, perception, decision making, or problem solving—relies on a whole network of brain regions rather than on a single region. Therefore, any relatively complex mental challenge will engage more than one part of the brain. Yet no single mental activity will engage the whole brain.

This is why the diversity of your mental life is key to your overall brain health. The more vigorous and varied your cognitive challenges, the more efficiently and effectively they'll protect your mind from decline. To return to the workout analogy: Imagine a physical gym. No single exercise machine will make you physically fit. Instead, you need a balanced and diverse workout regimen.

You have probably always assumed that crossword puzzles and sudoku are good for you, and they are. But your cognitive workout will benefit more from a greater variety of exercises, particularly if these exercises have been selected with some knowledge of how the brain works.

The puzzle selection for *Brain Games*™ has been guided by these considerations—with knowledge of the brain and the roles played by its different parts in the overall orchestra of your mental life. We aimed to assemble as wide a range of puzzles as possible in order to offer the brain a full workout.

There is no single magic pill to protect or enhance your mind, but vigorous, regular, and diverse mental activity is the closest thing to it. Research indicates that people engaged in mental activities as a result of their education and vocation are less likely to develop dementia as they age. In fact, many of these people demonstrate impressive mental alertness well into their eighties and nineties.

What's more, this "magic pill" need not be bitter. You can engage in activities that are both good for your brain *and* fun. Different kinds of puzzles engage different aspects of your mind, and you can assemble them all into a cognitive-workout regimen. Variety is the name of the game—that's the whole idea! In each cognitive workout session, have fun by mixing puzzles of different kinds. This book offers you enough puzzle variety to make this possible.

When it comes to difficulty level, welcome challenging puzzles. Don't assume they're beyond your ability without giving them your best shot first. To be effective as a mental workout, the puzzles you choose should not be too easy or too difficult. An overly easy puzzle will not stimulate your brain, just as a leisurely walk in the park is not an efficient way to condition your heart. You need mental exertion. On the other hand, an overly difficult puzzle will just frustrate you and discourage you from moving forward. So it is important to find the "challenge zone" that is appropriate for you. This may vary from person to person and from puzzle type to puzzle type. Here, too, the gym analogy applies. Different people will benefit most from different exercise machines and weight levels.

So we have tried to offer a range of difficulty for the various puzzle types. Try different puzzles to find the starting level appropriate for you. Soon, your puzzle-cracking ability will improve, and you may find that puzzles you once found too hard are now within your grasp.

Have Fun While Stretching Your Mind

The important thing is to have fun while doing something good for you. Puzzles can be engaging, absorbing, and even addictive. An increasing number of people make regular physical exercise part of their daily routines and miss it when circumstances prevent them from exercising. These habitual gym-goers know that strenuous effort is something to look forward to, not to avoid. Similarly, you will strengthen your mental muscle by actively challenging it. Don't put the puzzle book down when the solution is not immediately apparent. By testing your mind you will discover the joy of a particular kind of accomplishment: watching your mental powers grow. You must have the feeling of mental effort and exertion in order to exercise your brain.

This brings us to the next issue. While all puzzles are good for you, the degree of their effectiveness as brain conditioners is not the same. Some puzzles only test your knowledge of facts. Such puzzles may be enjoyable and useful to a degree, but they're not as useful in conditioning your brain as are the puzzles that require you to transform and manipulate information or do something with it by logic, multistep inference, mental rotation, planning, and so on. These latter puzzles are more likely to give you the feeling of mental exertion, of "stretching your mind," and they are also better for your brain health. You can use this feeling as a useful, though inexact, assessment of a puzzle's effectiveness as a brain conditioner.

Try to select puzzles in a way that complements, rather than duplicates, your job-related activities. If your profession involves dealing with words (e.g., an English teacher), try to emphasize spatial puzzles. If you are an engineer dealing with diagrams, focus on verbal puzzles. If your job is relatively devoid of mental challenges of any kind, mix several types of puzzles in equal proportions.

Cognitive decline frequently sets in with ageing. It often affects certain kinds of memory and certain aspects of attention and decision making. So as you age, it is particularly important to introduce cognitive exercise into your lifestyle to counteract any possible cognitive decline. But cognitive exercise is also important for the young and the middle-aged. We live in a world that depends increasingly on the brain more than on brawn. It is important to be sharp in order to get ahead in your career and to remain at the top of your game.

How frequently should you exercise your mind and for how long? Think in terms of an ongoing lifestyle change and not just a short-term commitment. Regularity is key, perhaps a few times a week for 30 to 45 minutes at a time. We've tried to make this easier by offering a whole series of *Brain Games*™ books. You can carry one of these puzzle books—your "cognitive workout gym"—in your briefcase, rucksack, or shopping bag. Our puzzles are intended to be fun, so feel free to fit them into your lifestyle in a way that enhances rather than disrupts it. Research shows that even a relatively brief regimen of vigorous cognitive activity often produces perceptible and lasting effects. But as with physical exercise, the results are best when cognitive exercise becomes a lifelong habit.

To help you gauge your progress, we have included two self-assessment questionnaires: one near the beginning of the book and one near the end. The questionnaires will guide you in rating your various cognitive abilities and any changes that you may experience as a

result of doing puzzles. Try to be as objective as possible when you fill out the questionnaires. Improving your cognitive skills in real-life situations is the most important practical outcome of exercising your mind, and you are in the best position to note whether and to what extent any improvement has taken place.

Now that you're aware of the great mental workout that awaits you in this book, we hope that you'll approach these puzzles with a sense of fun. If you have always been a puzzle fan, we offer a great rationale for indulging your passion! You have not been wasting your time by cracking challenging puzzles. Far from it! You have been training and improving your mind.

So, whether you are a new or seasoned puzzle-solver, enjoy your brain workout—and get smarter as you go!

ASSESS YOUR BRAIN

You are about to do something very smart: Embark on a set of exercises to improve your mind. But before you begin, take a moment to fill out this self-assessment questionnaire. It is for your own benefit, so you know how well your brain works before you challenge it with *Brain Games*™ puzzles. Then you will be able to track any changes in your mental performance and discover the ways in which you have improved.

The questions below are designed to test your skills in the areas of memory, problem solving, creative thinking, attention, language, and more. Please reflect on each question, and rate your responses on a 5-point scale, where 5 equals "excellent" and 1 equals "very poor." Then tally up your scores, and check out the categories at the bottom of the next page to learn how to sharpen your brain.

1. You go to a large shopping centre with a list of different errands to run. Once inside, you realize you've forgotten to bring your list. How likely are you to get everything you need?

    1   2   3   4   5

2. You've made an appointment with a doctor in an unfamiliar part of town. You printed out a map and directions, but once on the road you find that one of the streets you need to take is closed for construction. How well can you use your directions to find an alternate route?

    1   2   3   4   5

3. You're nearly finished with a project when your boss changes the focus of the assignment but not the due date. How well can you juggle the work to accommodate the change?

    1   2   3   4   5

4. How well can you remember everything you had for lunch the last three days?

    1   2   3   4   5

5. You're driving to a new place. You need to concentrate on the directions, but the radio is on and your passenger wants to have a conversation. Can you devote enough attention to get to your location, chat with your passenger, and not miss the traffic report on the radio?

    1   2   3   4   5

6. You're working on an assignment with a tight deadline, but your brother keeps calling to ask questions about the holiday you're taking together. Rate your ability to stay on task without getting distracted.

    1   2   3   4   5

7. How good are you at remembering important dates, such as birthdays or anniversaries? (If you forget your anniversary, you're not just in the doghouse—you'll have to deduct points.)

1   2   3   4   5

8. When taking a family holiday, how good are you at fitting your family's luggage and supplies into the boot? Can you plan in advance the layout of the suitcases, or do you find yourself packing and unpacking several times on your departure date?

1   2   3   4   5

9. You have a long shopping list for the supermarket but only have £30. How good are you at adding up the cost of essential items in your head so you don't go over once you get to the checkout?

1   2   3   4   5

10. You're hosting a reception, and you need to create a seating chart. You have to consider such factors as the available seating at each table, the importance of the guest, and the interpersonal relationships among the guests. How good are you at using logic to work out these complex seating arrangements?

1   2   3   4   5

10–25 Points:
Are You Ready to Make a Change?
Remember, it's never too late to improve your brain health! A great way to start is to work puzzles on a regular basis, and you've taken the first step by picking up this book. Choose a different type of puzzle each day, or do a variety of them daily to help strengthen memory, focus attention, and improve logic and problem solving.

26–40 Points:
Building Your Mental Muscle
You're no mental slouch, but there's room to sharpen your mind! Choose puzzles that will challenge you, especially the types of puzzles you might not like as much or would normally avoid. Remember, doing a puzzle can be the mental equivalent of doing sit-ups or squats: While they might not be your first choice of activity, you'll definitely like the results!

41–50 Points:
View from the Top
Congratulations! You're keeping your brain in tip-top shape. To maintain this level of mental fitness, keep challenging yourself by working puzzles every day. Like the rest of the body's muscles, your mental strength can decline if you don't use it. So choose to keep your brain strong and active. You're at the summit—now you just have to stay to enjoy the view!

Rhyme Time

Answer each clue below with a pair of rhyming words. The numbers that follow each clue indicate how many letters are in each word. For example, "Angry child (3, 3)" would be "hot tot."

1. Angry child (3, 3): _____

2. Crimson luge (3, 4): _____

3. Spot above the king in a straight (3, 5): _____

4. Bakery's inedible display item (4, 4): _____

5. Rear ribs (4, 4): _____

6. Where Goldilocks sat (4, 5): _____

7. Letters to the editor (4, 5): _____

8. Humorous Monopoly currency (5, 5): _____

9. Battle opener (5, 5): _____

10. Runt of the litter (5, 5): _____

Trivia on the Brain

Thousands of scientists study the brain; they are called neuroscientists. There are also many scientists who study computers. The scientists who study computers understand how computers work. But neuroscientists understand very little about the brain. They believe there is more they don't know than they do know about it.

Answers on page 170.

Finding You

Ignoring spaces and punctuation, underline all 12 occurrences of the consecutive letters Y-O-U in the paragraph below.

Young Yoda found a yo-yo under your Christmas tree. He tried to use it, but he looked like a monkey out of his tree. After hitting his head, he called his youthful friend Yoric and said, "Hurry, ouch!" Yoric rode the Tokyo Underground all the way to Youngstown, whistling the ditty "O Ulysses." "You're in luck, Yoda," said Yoric, "I'm a yo-yo user, too." Yoric taught Yoda to yo-yo, and in appreciation Yoda took some candy out and gave it to his friend.

Sudoku

LOGIC

Use deductive logic to complete the grid so that each row, each column, and each 3×3 box contains the numbers 1 through 9 in some order. The solution is unique.

3	5	1	7	8	9	2	6	4
4	7	2	6	3	5	8	9	1
6	9	8	1	4	2	7	3	5
2	6	4	9		3	5		8
9	3	5	4		8	6		2
1	8	7	5	6	2	9	4	3
5	4	9	8			3	2	6
7	2	6	3	5	4	1	8	9
8	1	3	2	9	6	4	5	7

Answers on page 170.

Gone Fishin'

Just about every week, John likes to cast a line or two in the river. But this week, everything seemed to go wrong. We count 6 things wrong with this picture. How many can you find?

Name Calling

ATTENTION   VISUAL SEARCH

Decipher the encoded word in the quip below using the numbers and letters on the phone pad. Remember that each number can stand for 3 or 4 possible letters.

1	2 ABC	3 DEF
4 GHI	5 JKL	6 MNO
7 PQRS	8 TUV	9 WXYZ
	0	

Money is the root of

all 9-3-2-5-8-4.

Answers on page 170.

Count on This!

Fill in the empty squares with numbers from 1 to 9. The numbers in each row must add up to the numbers in the right-hand column. The numbers in each column must add up to the numbers on the bottom line. The numbers in each corner-to-corner diagonal must add up to the numbers in the upper and lower right corners.

				15
1		7		23
		3		23
6	4		9	27
	2		5	10
17	22	19	25	21

Word Ladder

Change just one letter on each line to go from the top word to the bottom word. Do not change the order of the letters. You must have a common English word at each step.

BALL

———

———

GAME

Answers on page 170.

Thirsty?

Every word listed is contained within this group of letters. The words can be found in a straight line horizontally, vertically, or diagonally. They may read either backward or forward.

BEER   JUICE   SODA

COFFEE   LEMONADE   SPORTS DRINK

COLA   MILK   TEA

GIN   SHAKE   WATER

HOT CHOCOLATE   SMOOTHIE   WINE

```
T Z R M K N K R Z N K E
K K Z L D B W T I K K T
N S L N M E M G L N R A
I M R I Y E T M K E E L
R O F J M R W J T Q D O
D O X Z T I K A D P A C
S T E Q N T W J L C N O
T H C E P P E R Q O O H
R I I D Z K D A J L M C
O E U M A H X D V A E T
P V J H C O F F E E L O
S L S P O P A D O S F H
```

Answers on page 170.

Quilt Quest

ATTENTION   VISUAL SEARCH

The small tricoloured pattern on the right appears exactly twice in the quilt shown below. Note that the pattern might appear rotated but not overlapped and/or mirrored in the quilt.

Hello, My Name Is Wrong

LOGIC   PROBLEM SOLVING

The meeting was about to start, the two guest speakers had not yet arrived, and Sally, the meeting planner, had a dilemma. She had filled out name tags for everyone but the speakers because she couldn't remember their names. All she knew was that their first names were Morey and Les, and their last names were Thyme and Munny. She decided to fill out three tags with the names Morey Thyme, Morey Munny, and Les Munny and hoped two of them were right. The guest speakers finally showed up and laughed when they saw the name tags. They promised not to tell Sally's boss that two of the name tags were wrong if she could tell them their real names. Sally needed the money from this job so she took her time and figured it out. What were the guests' names?

Answers on pages 170–171.

Word Jigsaw

Fit the pieces into the frame to form words reading across and down crossword-style. There is no need to rotate any of the pieces; they will fit as shown, with each piece used exactly once.

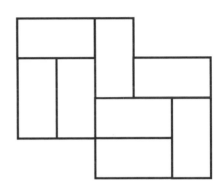

Geometric Shapes

Divide the grid into smaller geometric shapes by drawing straight lines either following the full grid lines or the full diagonals of the square cells. Each formed shape must have exactly one symbol inside, which represents it but might not look identical to it. (In other words, a triangle that you draw must have only a triangle symbol within it, although the drawn triangle and the triangle symbol may look slightly different.) Hint: The trapezoid has two sides parallel, but its other two sides are not parallel.

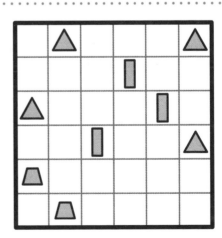

Answers on page 171.

Where Are the Animals?

Find the names of 2 animals in each group of letters. The letters in each name are in their proper order. We've done one for you.

1. DOCAGT   DOG   CAT

2. SEKLUNKK   _____   _____

3. DEOWERL   _____   _____

4. FOSNAXKE   _____   _____

5. WHOORLSEF   _____   _____

6. RELAEBPHABINTT   _____   _____

7. TILIGONER   _____   _____

8. MEONAGKLEYE   _____   _____

9. SWEHAALLE   _____   _____

10. PEAREROLT   _____   _____

Trivia on the Brain

Your mind is basically a seven-pound ball of malleable flesh. Every bit of it crackles with billions of little switches called *synapses*. These are the points at which your brain's nerve cells exchange ions. We call this "thinking." The more synaptic connections you form in your mind, the more you know. As you age, these connections begin to fray. We call this "forgetting."

Answers on page 171.

Flying High

Unscramble the names of these common birds, then use the numbered squares to solve the second puzzle, a related idiom.

COANFL

RIOBN

CAALINRD

NAARYC

BIRDULEB

WOCR

EGLAE

WSROPRA

GASLIRNT

Answers on page 171.

Time Capsule

LANGUAGE   LOGIC

Cryptograms are messages in substitution code. For example, THE SMART CAT might become FVO QWGDF JGF if **F** is substituted for **T, V** for **H, O** for **E,** and so on. Break the code to reveal the quote below and its author.

Hint: Look for repeated letters. **E, T, A, O, N, R,** and **I** are the most often used letters. A single letter is usually **A** or **I;** OF, IS, and IT are common 2-letter words; THE and AND are common 3-letter words.

"G OCPN NI U BCZNUSBUPN NQUN

ZCBLCZ 'DBCURVUZN UN UPH NGYC,'

ZI G IBXCBCX VBCPKQ NIUZN XSBGPA

NQC BCPUGZZUPKC."   —ZNCLCP OBGAQN

Jumbled Idiom

LANGUAGE

Most idioms are figures of speech that aren't meant to be taken literally. If someone "kicks the bucket," it means the person died—no bucket actually got kicked. In this puzzle, though, the illustration is literal. It's meant to give you a clue to the idiom, which has been jumbled into an anagram. Figuring out the picture can help you figure out the idiomatic phrase.

FAUCET CHIMES

Answers on page 171.

Word Columns

LANGUAGE   PLANNING   SPATIAL REASONING

Find the hidden phrase by using the letters directly below each of the blank squares. Each letter is used only once.

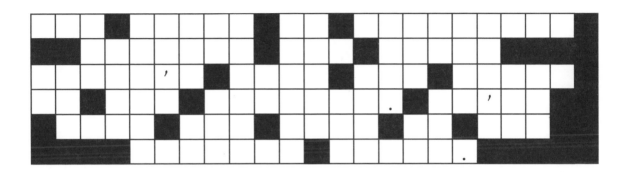

```
        p       n   k
        a   o f h   w s   n   o u
    t a k n a u n e   i h p t h w t e t l s
i n e s c n t e l g i n e r e i W r g e n
T h b t e l o t f i t e e s p t l n o i l g
d o e e h e a s e e r h e i l e e o n i t e
```

Name Calling

ATTENTION   VISUAL SEARCH

Decipher the encoded word in the quip below using the numbers and letters on the phone pad. Remember that each number can stand for 3 or 4 possible letters.

1	2 ABC	3 DEF
4 GHI	5 JKL	6 MNO
7 PQRS	8 TUV	9 WXYZ
	0	

4-7-2-8-4-8-9 always wins.

Answers on page 171.

Seven Slices

PROBLEM SOLVING   SPATIAL VISUALISATION

Divide the large circle with three straight lines so that there is only one small circle in each segment.

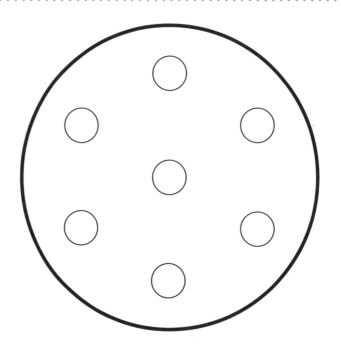

Game On!

LANGUAGE   LOGIC   PROBLEM SOLVING

Fill each square of the grid with 1 of the 4 letters of the word GAME so that each row, each column, and each of the 2 long diagonals contains all 4 letters exactly once. We've inserted four letters to get you started.

			A
		M	
A			
			G

Answers on page 171.

Rhyme Time

Answer each clue below with a pair of rhyming words. The numbers that follow each clue indicate how many letters are in each word. For example, "Body of water filled with skates (3, 3)" would be "ray bay."

1. Body of water filled with skates (3, 3): _____

2. Celestial object at a distance (3, 4): _____

3. Appellation that can lead to mistaken identity (4, 4): _____

4. Abode in Italy's capital (4, 4): _____

5. Subdued reaction to a joke (4, 5): _____

6. It may make a runner miss the base (4, 5): _____

Word Jigsaw

Fit the pieces into the frame to form common, uncapitalised words reading across and down crossword-style. There's no need to rotate the pieces; they'll fit as shown, with each piece used exactly once.

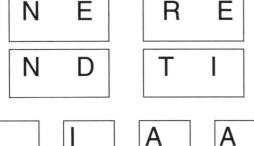

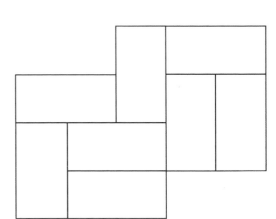

Answers on page 171.

Mirror, Mirror

There's no trick here, only a challenge: Draw the mirror image of each of these familiar objects. You may find it harder than you think!

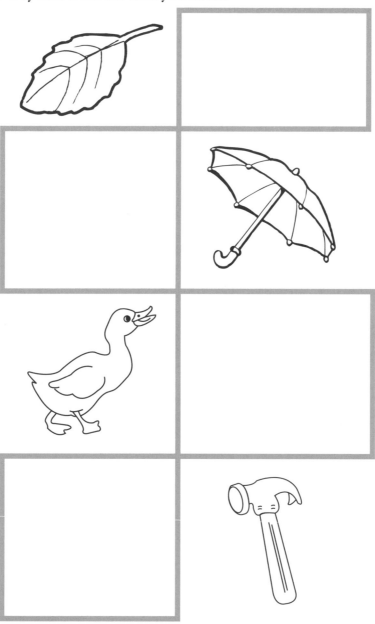

Fish Fantasy

This tank is just swimming with fish. Can you find the 2 that match?

Answers on page 172.

Backyard Barbecue

LANGUAGE

Throw some shrimp (and some anagrams!) on the barbie! Within the sentences below are 10 jumbled phrases. Each is an anagram (rearrangement) of a word or phrase that helps complete the story. Can you decipher all 10?

The kids were playing on the WET SIGNS, Uncle Frank and Jack from next door were playing a game of HOSE SHORES, and it was time for the grill. The TOAST PIE had been dusted off, and Kristen, their teen-ager, was stretched out on the EAGLE CUSHION, checking out her SHORE COOP in her favorite GAIN MAZE. The RUM LABEL offered some shade, and it was time for the announcement: "NO HBO CONCERT!" This was followed by PRESCRIBE MAD HUB and a genial reminder TO CHOKE SKIS!

The Good Book

ANALYSIS CREATIVE THINKING

Can you determine the missing letter in this progression?

$$M, \_\_, L, J$$

Answers on page 172.

The Fruit Vendor's Cart

Help a fruit vendor with an overturned fruit cart to gather all the fruit and put it back on his cart. The list below contains each kind of fruit he had on his cart. The grid represents the only way the cart can be organized to hold all the fruit. Put each word in its proper place so the vendor can get on his way.

APPLE	FIG	PEACH
APRICOT	GRAPE	PEAR
AVOCADO	LEMON	STRAWBERRY
BANANA	LIME	TANGERINE
CHERRY	ORANGE	

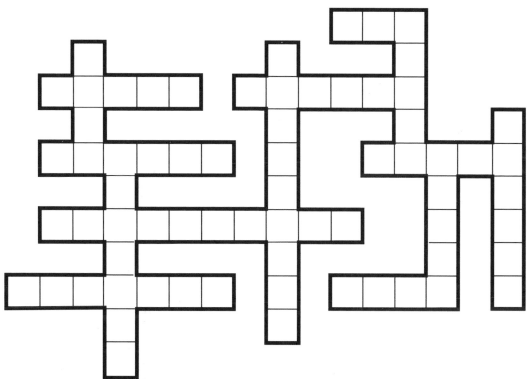

Answers on page 172.

Max and Mitch

LANGUAGE

Oops, we meant *Mix and Match*. But that's what happens when those anagram imps stir up the letters in a word. Can you unscramble the phrases listed below and match the results to their musical pictures?

1. CIRCULATE TIGER

4. IOTA NUMBER

2. HOAX OPENS

5. A CHARM ION

3. MOM UTTERED "JAR"

6. ID RACCOON

A

B

C

D

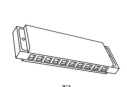
E

F

Geometric Shapes

LOGIC   SPATIAL REASONING

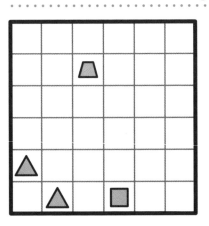

Divide the grid into smaller geometric shapes by drawing straight lines either following the full grid lines or the full diagonals of the square cells. Each formed shape must have exactly one symbol inside, which represents it but might not look identical to it. (In other words, a triangle you draw must have only a triangle symbol within it, although the drawn triangle and the triangle symbol may look slightly different.) Hint: The trapezoid has two sides parallel, but its other two sides are not parallel.

Answers on page 172.

Layer by Layer

Sixteen sheets of paper—all equal in size and shape—were piled on top of a table. Number the sheets from top to bottom, with numbers 1 through 16.

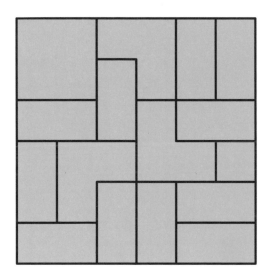

Word Ladder

Change just one letter on each line to go from the top word to the bottom word. Do not change the order of the letters. You must have a common English word at each step.

REAL

_____

_____

SHAM

Answers on page 172.

Fitting Words

LANGUAGE   LOGIC   PLANNING

In this miniature crossword, the clues are listed randomly and are numbered for convenience only. It is up to you to figure out the placement of the 9 answers. To help you out, we've inserted the letter **I** in the grid, and this is the *only* occurrence of that letter in the completed puzzle.

Clues

1. Capital city of France
2. Member of a cast
3. Learning method
4. _____ and carrots
5. Vassal
6. Ledge
7. Curved part of the foot
8. Wear away
9. False god

Name Calling

ATTENTION   VISUAL SEARCH

Decipher the encoded word in the quip below using the numbers and letters on the phone pad. Remember that each number can stand for 3 or 4 possible letters.

1	2 ABC	3 DEF
4 GHI	5 JKL	6 MNO
7 PQRS	8 TUV	9 WXYZ
	0	

The hardest thing

when learning how to

7-5-2-8-3 is probably the ice.

Answers on page 172.

Layer by Layer

Twelve sheets of paper—all equal in size and shape—were piled on top of a table. Number the sheets from top to bottom, with numbers 1 through 12.

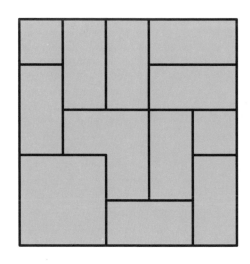

First Song

An anagram is a word or phrase in which the letters are rearranged to create another word or phrase. The anagrams below name a well-known U.S. song and its genre.

1. PLANTER BANNED GRASS

2. NOT A THIN MAN

Answers on page 173.

At the Movies

ATTENTION   LANGUAGE   VISUAL SEARCH

Every word listed below is contained within the group of letters on page 33. The words can be found in a straight line horizontally, vertically, or diagonally. The words may read either backward or forward.

ACADEMY AWARD	CO-STAR	PREVIEW
ACTION	DIRECTOR	PRODUCER
ACTOR	DOCUMENTARY	REVIEWER
ACTRESS	EGRESS	SCI-FI
AISLES	EPIC	SCREEN
ARCADE	FEATURE	SCRIPT
BALCONY	FILM NOIR	SEATS
BOX OFFICE	GENRE	SEQUEL
CAMERA	INDIE	SODA
CANDY	MULTIPLEX	SOUND
CAST	MUSICAL	STUBS
CLASSIC	OPENING	USHER
COMEDY	PREQUEL	WRITER

Y C W A C A D E M Y A W A R D
N A Z F E A T U R E P I C O I
O N C G F I L M N O I R C Z R
C D M T L T P I R C S U A M E
L Y S C I F I R S W M Y S U C
A O J P R O T C A E S S T S T
B P L E I D N I N L Q O Y I O
O E E R X Y S T U B S U D C R
X N U E C L A S S I C N E A E
O I Q W R R Z S S E W D M L C
F N E E Y N C O S T A R O U U
F G R I A R E M A C Z T C S D
I Y P V E T E G R E S S S H O
C S S E R T C A I S L E S E R
E V N R E T I R W E I V E R P

Trivia on the Brain

Your body is being constantly controlled by your brain, keeping you breathing and your heart beating at all times.

Answers on page 173.

Shall We Dance?

Ever hear of the allemande, the Bihu dance of India, or the chacarera of Argentina? Neither had we until we looked into this puzzle. We haven't included those exotic steps—we think you'll know these dances. Decipher the anagrams (rearrangements) below, and match them to the pictures.

1. FLANK COED

2. DECAL BY LEN

3. EARNED BACK

4. SQUANDER ACE

5. CALF OMEN

6. CADET NAP

A.

B.

C.

D.

E.

F.

Answers on page 173.

34

Star Power

ATTENTION   LOGIC

Fill in each of the empty squares in the grid so that each star is surrounded by numbers 1 through 8 with no repeats.

2	7	1	★	2	8	4
8	★	4	8	7	★	6
6	5	3	★	5	1	3
8	★	1	2	6	★	2
2	4	7	★	8	4	7
★		5	3	4	★	★

Word Ladder

LANGUAGE   PLANNING

Change just one letter on each line to go from the top word to the bottom word. Do not change the order of the letters.

STARS

_____ gaze intently

_____ portion

_____

SHINE

Answers on page 173.

A Bit Askew

Can you make your way
through this maze?

The But-Not Game

The object of The But-Not Game is to uncover the element common to each
statement.

Carol likes felines but not cats.

Carol likes halibut but not flounder.

Carol likes palaces but not castles.

So . . . what does Carol like?

Answers on page 173.

Mirror, Mirror

There's no trick here, only a challenge: Draw the mirror image of each of these familiar objects. You may find it harder than you think!

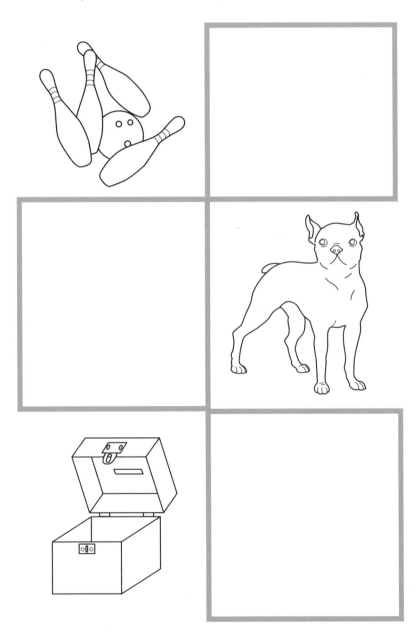

See Your Name in Print!

This puzzle is so amazing we can hardly catch our breath. Just mentally assemble the letter parts, and they'll spell your name! Sorry, we can't reveal the amazing 23rd-century technology behind this wizardry. By the way: One or more letter parts may have been rotated—a small obstacle to the fun of seeing your name in print!

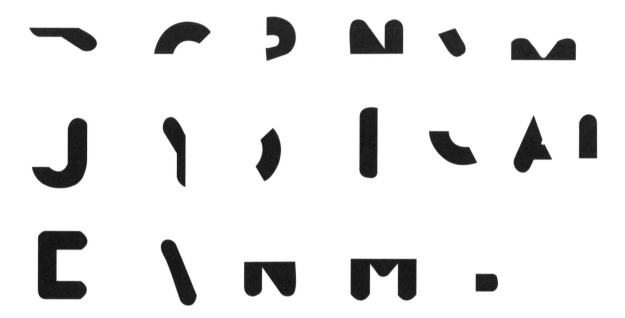

It's Old

ANALYSIS   CREATIVE THINKING

Can you determine the first letter in this progression?

____, E, L, N, D

Answers on page 173.

Rhyme Time

Answer each clue below with a pair of rhyming words. The numbers that follow each clue indicate how many letters are in each word. For example, "Key to the poem's secret message (3, 4)" would be "ode code."

1. Key to the poem's secret message (3, 4): _____

2. Long-lasting winter ailment (3, 4): _____

3. Stolen pleasure boat (3, 5): _____

4. Atlantic wave (5, 6): _____

5. Dangerous place for a stroll (4, 4): _____

6. Hardware store promo (4, 4): _____

7. Scabbard hanger (5, 4): _____

8. Little heist (5, 4): _____

9. Missing color (5, 4): _____

10. The fish always bite it (5, 4 *or* 4, 4): _____

11. Gymnastic group (4, 4): _____

12. Robin Hood, to his merry men (5, 5): _____

13. Short poem (5, 5): _____

14. Mediocre dessert (4, 6): _____

15. Some teen swimmers practice here (6, 4): _____

Answers on page 174.

Crazy Mixed-Up Letters

Make 3 different 7-letter words by rearranging all of the letters shown here.

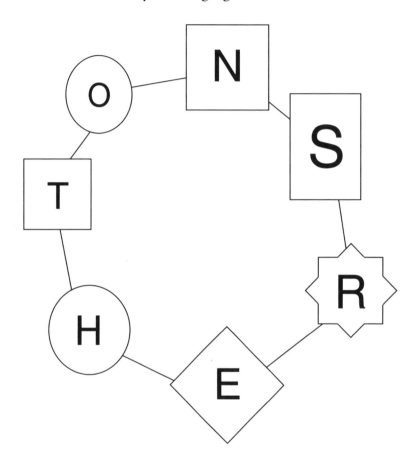

Trivia on the Brain

Your amygdala is your brain's alarm system. Depending on which area is stimulated, your body will experience either a "fight" response or a "flight" response.

Answers on page 174.

Let's Make Some Music

The letters in the word UKULELE can be found in boxes 12, 16, 19, and 22, but not necessarily in that order. Similarly, the letters in all the other listed musical instruments can be found in the boxes indicated. Your task is to insert all the letters of the alphabet into the grid. If you do this correctly, the names of 2 more instruments will be revealed in the shaded squares.

Hint: Compare BANJO and BASSOON to get the values of **J** and **S**. Then compare BASSOON and DOUBLE BASS to get the value of **N**.

BANJO: 5, 6, 7, 8, 21

BASSOON: 5, 6, 7, 20, 21

DOUBLE BASS: 5, 7, 14, 16, 19, 20, 21, 22

FLUTE: 10, 13, 16, 19, 22

OCARINA: 4, 5, 6, 7, 15, 23

ORGAN: 1, 5, 6, 7, 15

PICCOLO: 3, 4, 7, 19, 23

SAXOPHONE: 2, 3, 5, 6, 7, 11, 20, 22

TIN WHISTLE: 2, 4, 6, 9, 10, 19, 20, 22

TRUMPET: 3, 10, 15, 16, 17, 22

UKULELE: 12, 16, 19, 22

VIOLA: 4, 5, 7, 19, 24

1	2	3	4	5	6	7	8	9	10	11	12	13

14	15	16	17	18	19	20	21	22	23	24	25	26
												Q

Answers on page 174.

Revving Your Motor

X-Hibit of X's

Within this picture is an "x-hibit" of things that begin with the letter "X." We count 3 things. How many can you find?

Sudoku

Use deductive logic to complete the grid so that each row, each column, and each 3×3 box contains the numbers 1 through 9 in some order. The solution is unique.

9	3	2	5	7	1	4	6	8
4	5	7	8	6	2	1	9	3
1	8	6	9	3	4	2	5	7
7	4	9	3	2	6	8	1	5
2	1	5	7	9	8	6	3	4
3	6	8	1	4	5	9	7	2
6	9	4	2	5	3	7	8	1
8	7	3	4	1	9	5	2	6
5	2	1	6	8	7	3	4	9

Answers on page 174.

Inching Along

Ignoring spaces and punctuation, underline all 14 occurrences of the consecutive letters I-N-C-H in the paragraph below.

In China, inchworms are used in a pinch when fishing for perch in channels. Zinc has also been used, especially if the perch in channels are susceptible to colds. One fisherman using inchworms caught so many perch, he had to clinch his boat to his truck with a winch and inch it up the bank. A goldfinch flew in his window and made him flinch, but he did nothing because in China it's against the law to lynch a finch.

Sum Fun

Fill in the empty squares with numbers from 1 through 9. The numbers in each row must add up to the totals in the right-hand column. The numbers in each column must add up to the totals on the bottom line. The numbers in each corner-to-corner diagonal must add up to the totals in the upper and lower right corners.

						30
9	3	5	4	7	3	31
2	1	2	8	2	8	23
1	6	4	1	9	3	24
7	3	7	2	1	6	26
4	9	8	6	4	5	36
8	5	9	5	7	1	35
31	27	35	26	30	26	21

Answers on page 174.

Between the Lines

LANGUAGE   LOGIC

Solve for the middle (undefined) word in each set. All three words in each set would appear on the same page in the dictionary, in the order given. Then use the four middle words to complete the quote at the bottom of the page.

Example: putter: *to work at random: tinker*
          puzzle
          pygmy: *small person of Africa*

1. a) __ __ __ d: *nutriment in solid form*

   b) __ __ o __

   c) __ __ __ t: *fraction of a yard*

2. a) __ r __ v __ : *a planting of fruit or nut trees*

   b) __ __ __ __ __

   c) __ __ __ __ __: *a deep, guttural, inarticulate sound*

3. a) w __ __ __ __ __ __ d: *to deduct from income*

   b) __ __ __ __ __ __ __ t

   c) __ __ __ __ __ __ __ n d: *to resist successfully*

4. a) __ __ __ c __: *to observe closely*

   b) __ __ t __ __

   c) __ __ t t: *lightbulb unit*

"_____s _____ _____ _____ing."

—*Thomas Fuller*

Answers on page 174.

Ubiquity of U's

There is a ubiquity of things that begin with **U** in this picture. We count 8. How many can you find?

Answers on page 174.

How Will You Conduct Yourself?

Every word listed is contained within this group of letters. The words can be found in a straight line horizontally, vertically, or diagonally. They may read either backward or forward.

ADAGIO	CLASSICAL	HARMONY	REST
ALLEGRO	CONCERTO	LEGATO	SCALE
BEAT	CONDUCTOR	MOVEMENT	SCORE
BRASS	ENCORE	MUSIC	STRINGS
CANTATA	ETUDE	ORCHESTRA	
CHORD	FORTE	PERCUSSION	

```
O  Y  T  D  P  C  L  Y  N  O  M  R  A  H  N
N  I  K  L  T  I  L  A  C  I  S  S  A  L  C
K  R  G  Y  N  S  T  H  C  A  N  T  A  T  A
D  K  M  A  R  U  W  L  D  P  A  C  L  N  N
H  H  G  N  D  M  N  D  M  E  L  E  R  V  R
P  T  F  S  S  A  R  B  B  B  G  D  S  O  K
E  C  O  N  C  E  R  T  O  A  N  C  T  T  M
R  N  O  R  C  H  E  S  T  R  A  C  X  O  E
C  O  Q  L  R  S  E  O  W  L  U  D  V  K  D
U  R  R  E  S  T  T  F  E  D  T  E  G  C  U
S  G  N  S  R  Q  K  R  N  R  M  B  H  H  T
S  E  C  O  C  F  H  O  I  E  O  F  J  O  E
I  L  F  N  L  O  C  D  N  N  H  C  B  R  M
O  L  F  Q  R  T  R  T  N  K  G  M  N  D  R
N  A  L  K  T  L  V  E  G  L  F  S  T  E  D
```

Answers on page 175.

Word Ladder

Change just 1 letter on each line to go from the top word to the bottom word. Do not change the order of the letters. You must have a common English word at each step.

BEAR

———

———

———

———

BULL

Count Down

32

Fill in the empty squares with numbers from 1 through 9. The numbers in each row must add up to the numbers in the right-hand column. The numbers in each column must add up to the numbers on the bottom line. The numbers in each corner-to-corner diagonal must add up to the numbers in the upper and lower right corners.

1		5		4	**23**
1		2		5	**20**
7	2	2	4		**23**
	8		7		**26**
9	9			2	**26**
21	**27**	**19**	**31**	**20**	**15**

Answers on page 175.

47

Tessellated Floor

Show how the 5 pieces can form the mosaic floor on the left. Pieces can be rotated but not overlapped or mirrored.

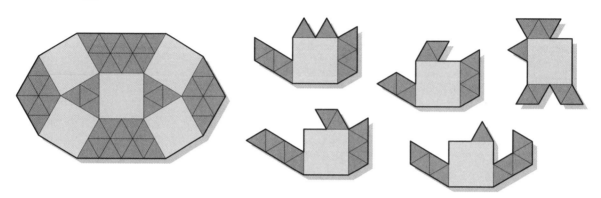

Word Jigsaw

LANGUAGE   SPATIAL PLANNING

Fit the pieces into the frame to form words reading across and down crossword-style. There is no need to rotate any of the pieces; they will fit as shown, with each piece used exactly once.

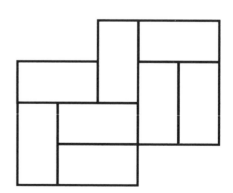

Answers on page 175.

Number Challenge

Fill in this crossword with numbers instead of letters. Use the clues to determine which of the numbers 1 through 9 belongs in each square. No zeros are used.

Across

1. A multiple of 7
3. A prime number
5. Consecutive digits, ascending
7. 700 more than 10-Across
8. Five different odd numbers, out of order
10. 10 more than 11-Across
11. A multiple of 5

Down

1. A multiple of 11
2. Five different odd numbers, out of order
3. A palindrome that is 8-Across minus 2-Down
4. The square of an even square
6. The first and last digits add up to the middle digit
8. A multiple of 11
9. A multiple of 3

1	2	■	3	4
5		6		
■	7			■
8				9
10		■	11	

Trivia on the Brain

After a limb is paralysed or amputated, most people can still feel sensations that seem to come from the limb. Some people even feel as if they can move their missing limb.

Answers on page 175.

Triple-Jointed

LOGIC   PLANNING   SPATIAL REASONING

Write each word or phrase below in the grid on the facing page. They only fit one way. For extra credit, determine what all these words have in common.

7 LETTERS

WELL-LIT

9 LETTERS

CHESS SETS

CLIFF FACE

FREE E-MAIL

STILL LIFE

10 LETTERS

DRESS SHIRT

FULL-LENGTH

GRASS SKIRT

SCOTT TUROW

SQUALL LINE

STIFF FINES

SWISS STEAK

YOU'LL LAUGH

11 LETTERS

CROSS SWORDS

MISS SCARLET

SEE EYE TO EYE

12 LETTERS

BRASS SECTION

BUSINESS SUIT

GLASS SLIPPER

SUCCESS STORY

WITNESS STAND

15 LETTERS

FOR GOODNESS SAKE

IN ALL LIKELIHOOD

IT'S A ZOO OUT THERE

16 LETTERS

SEAMLESS STOCKING

Trivia on the Brain

The central nervous system is involved in most functions of your body. These include touch and sensation, bladder control, and muscle movement. Your spinal cord, which is part of this system, carries nerve messages to and from your brain.

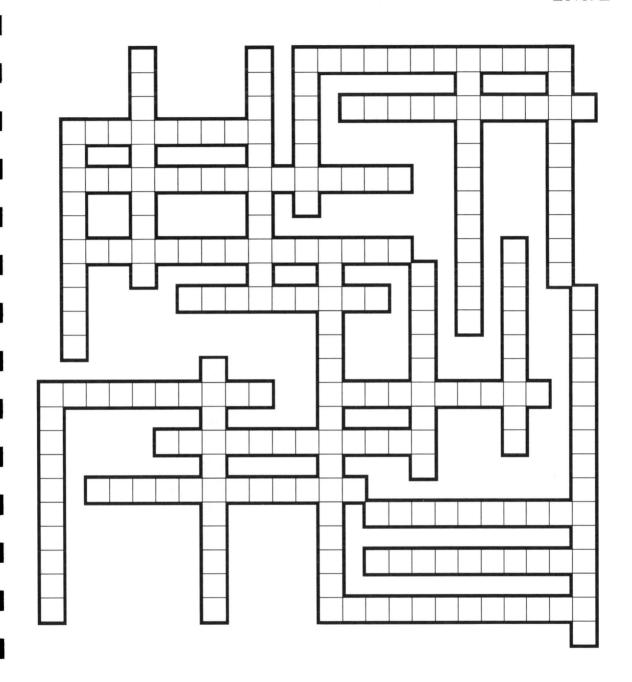

Extra-Credit Answer:_____

Answers on page 175.

Letters to Numbers

COMPUTATION | PROBLEM SOLVING

Each letter represents a different number from 1 through 9. Use the clues to help you put the numbers in their places within the grid.

A	B	C
D	E	F
G	H	J

Clues:

1. $G \times G = F + H$
2. $B \times G \times J = A$
3. $B \times D = D$
4. $D + D = G + J$
5. $E + H = B + C + F$

Hint: Since $D + D = G + J$, $G + J$ must equal an even number.

Copycats

ATTENTION | VISUAL SEARCH

Which cat appears 4 times? Keep in mind that the image may be mirrored.

Answers on pages 175–176.

Animal Farm

Welcome to the Mixed-Up Menagerie, a veritable zoo of friendly, if somewhat tangled, critters. You can't get in here unless you've found a suitable disguise. See that little SNEAK over there? Oops, he's really a SNAKE. How many more anagrammed (rearranged) beasts can you uncover?

Over there is the NEED I ERR, who thinks he's a caribou and doesn't like it when the SHOPPERS RAG lands on his head. You wouldn't want to trifle with the GLARING BEET, a feline refugee from a circus act. The giant NEAT HELP is about the only one who doesn't seem intimidated by him. The MESH TAR and LEG RIB appear to enjoy running inside that little Ferris wheel, while the GOLF DISH tend to prefer the safety of the pond. Meanwhile, the EGO NIP flutters around dropping "presents" on everyone, even the graceful African PALE NOTE.

Trivia on the Brain

Even though it's called phantom pain, the pain coming from a missing limb is not imagined. The feeling of pain is generated by the brain, so it is the same feeling as pain felt anywhere else on the body.

Answers on page 176.

Match-Up Twins

ATTENTION

These 10 hexagons may look identical at first glance, but they're not. They can be divided into 5 pairs of identical designs. Can you match them up?

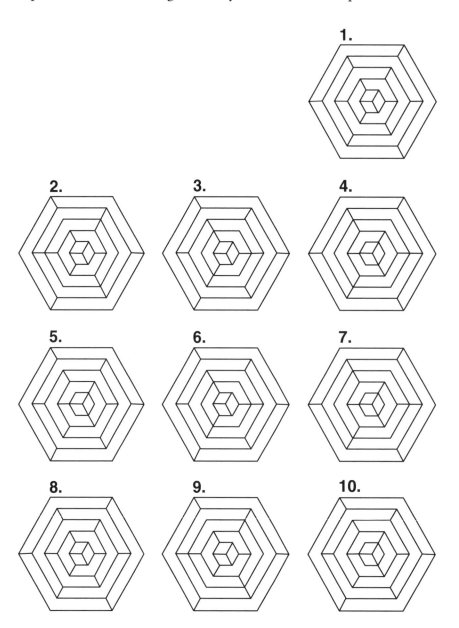

Answers on page 176.

Rhyme Time

Answer each clue below with a pair of rhyming words. The numbers that follow each clue indicate how many letters are in each word. For example, "Stingy monarch (4, 5)" would be "mean queen."

1. Stingy monarch (4, 5): _____

2. Fun 24 hours (4, 3): _____

3. Identification problem (4, 4): _____

4. Dentist's order (4, 5): _____

5. Judge's irritation (4, 5): _____

6. Extremely unshaven (4, 5): _____

7. Equal thirds, perhaps (4, 5): _____

8. Beau's noncommittal response (5, 4): _____

9. Vocalist's faux pas (5, 4): _____

10. Main gripe (5, 5): _____

11. Tennis (5, 5): _____

12. Furniture item in storage (5, 5): _____

13. Seem close (6, 4): _____

14. Scheme to sell fake designer Etons (6, 6): _____

15. The case of the missing taper (6, 7): _____

Answers on page 176.

Word Columns

LANGUAGE · PLANNING · SPATIAL REASONING

Find the hidden phrase by using the letters directly below each of the blank squares. Each letter in a column is used only once in the squares above it.

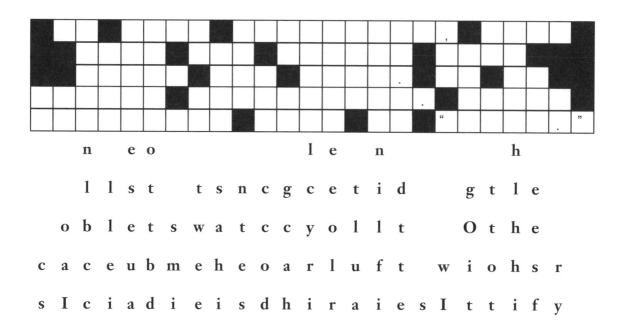

Back at You

CREATIVE THINKING · LOGIC

Place it in a picture frame, and it shows a picture of you. Turn it upside down, and it still shows a picture of you right side up. What is it?

Answers on page 176.

Grab Bag

The anagram imp has been at it again! He's scrambled the names of these items just for the fun of it. Decipher the anagrams (rearrangements) below, and match them to the correct pictures.

1. NO BOWLEGS

2. DESTROY OIL

3. RADIANCE FIGS

4. A BISON

5. HOWL FIBS

A.

B.

C.

D.

E.

Answers on page 176.

Fitting Words

LANGUAGE   LOGIC   PLANNING

In this miniature crossword, the clues are listed randomly and are numbered for convenience only. It is up to you to figure out the placement of the 9 answers. To help you out, we've inserted one letter in the grid, and this is the only occurrence of that letter in the completed puzzle.

Clues

1. Visibility problem
2. Peru's capital
3. Dumbfound
4. Racetrack shape
5. Waikiki welcome
6. Bundles of hay
7. Show horse
8. Competitor
9. Beers

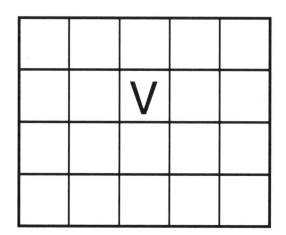

Word Ladder

LANGUAGE   PLANNING

Change just one letter on each line to go from the top word to the bottom word. Do not change the order of the letters. You must have a common English word at each step.

HAIR

_____

_____

_____

BALD

Answers on page 176.

City Sites

Can you match these famous sites to their respective cities?

La Scala	New Orleans
Taj Mahal	London
Basin Street	Beijing
Left Bank	Tokyo
Colosseum	Paris
Piccadilly Circus	Havana
Kremlin	Milan
Forbidden City	Agra
Ginza	Rome
Moro Castle	Moscow

Tamagram

Find an expression to define the picture below, and then rearrange the letters of it to form a 9-letter word. LLL, for example, is THREE L'S, which is an anagram of SHELTER.

END

Answers on page 176.

Quilt Quest

ATTENTION

VISUAL SEARCH

The small tricoloured pattern at far right appears exactly twice in the quilt shown here. Find both instances. Note that the pattern might appear rotated but not overlapped and/or mirrored in either instance.

Word Jigsaw

LANGUAGE

SPATIAL PLANNING

Fit the pieces into the frame to form words reading across and down crossword-style. There is no need to rotate any of the pieces; they will fit as shown, with each piece used exactly once.

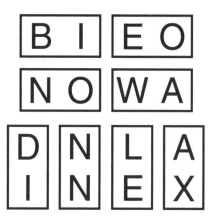

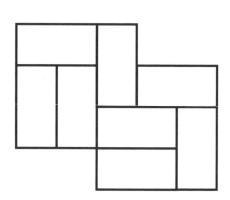

Answers on page 177.

ATTENTION

LANGUAGE   VISUAL SEARCH

Bears Repeating

Every word listed is contained within this group of letters. The words can be found in a straight line horizontally, vertically, or diagonally. They may read either backward or forward.

BLACK

BROWN

GRIZZLY

KODIAK

PANDA

POLAR

SLOTH

SPECTACLED

SUN

```
Y  G  C  H  K  X  K  K  D  D
T  D  R  K  T  N  U  S  L  E
T  J  D  I  X  O  B  L  R  L
P  G  R  T  Z  L  L  K  H  C
K  T  H  Y  A  Z  A  S  Y  A
K  A  K  C  P  I  L  N  B  T
F  D  K  M  D  B  T  Y  R  C
C  N  P  O  L  A  R  R  O  E
Y  A  K  R  D  X  K  T  W  P
G  P  K  C  L  K  Z  P  N  S
```

Wacky Wordy

CREATIVE THINKING   LANGUAGE

Can you "read" the phrase below?

BLOUNECMOEON

Answers on page 177.

Bungle Gym

LANGUAGE

If he builds it, they will come…mainly to laugh! Can you decipher the anagrams below without breaking anything?

We wanted to build a jungle gym for our 5-year-old and his playmates, so we called a carpenter. We wanted it made of wood and plastic, so we should have had a clue when he asked for his BROW CLOTH. Things went downhill after that. He didn't know how to use the CRUCIAL WARS, and we got a little worried when he shouted, "I WAS CHAN!" This was followed by "I need my WEB ATLAS." Later he went back to his truck for some LOGIC SPRINKLE. As you can see, the result was less than ideal. "You're outta here!" shouted my husband, brandishing his CAR BROW.

Alternate Universe?

LOGIC

Mr. Bee Zarro claims to come from a parallel universe where afternoon comes before noon, tomorrow comes before yesterday, and later comes before now. But you don't need to go to a parallel universe to see the same things happen. Where can you see this here on Earth?

Answers on page 177.

Born in 1875 `LOGIC`

Handsome Hank was born in 1875 and is still alive today. He's not the oldest man in the world. In fact, he's in perfect health and doesn't look a day over 25. How does Handsome Hank manage to look like he swims daily in the fountain of youth even though he was born in 1875?

Sudoku `LOGIC`

Use deductive logic to complete the grid so that each row, each column, and each 3×3 box contains the numbers 1 through 9 in some order. The solution is unique.

8	2	3	5	6	4	9	1	7
6	7	4	3	9	1	5	8	2
5	9	1	7	2	8	6	3	4
2	4	6	1	7	9	8	5	3
1	8	9	4	5	3	2	7	6
7	3	5	2	8	6	4	9	1
4	5	8	6	3	7	1	2	9
3	6	2	9	1	5	7	4	8
9	1	7	8	4	2	3	6	5

Answers on page 177.

Horsing Around

Every phrase listed below is contained within the group of letters on the next page. They can be found in a straight line horizontally, vertically, or diagonally. They may read either backward or forward.

As an added challenge, see if you can figure out the theme of this puzzle.

CRAZY QUILT

DARK SHADOWS

DEAD RINGER

GIFT OF GAB

HIGH AND LOW

HOBBY SHOP

IRON MAIDEN

ONE AT A TIME

PACK RAT

RACE RELATIONS

RIVER PHOENIX

ROCKING CHAIR

SAW EYE TO EYE

SEA CHANGE

STUD POKER

WAR AND PEACE

WILD WEST

WORK OF ART

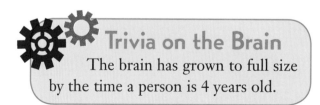

Trivia on the Brain
The brain has grown to full size by the time a person is 4 years old.

```
        S E R X P S W E R E S
        S A I O T G C I O N S
      T R H W U C A I A L T B E
  R G N I I D E E K H F N D O W C I
  T A H E P V P Y O I E T N W L W S
  O R C O D D E B E G N E O O E W D
  S R K E N I B R N T A G T F O S T
  H E E A R Y A A P T O H C D G L T
  R I R G S E H M A H E E A H I A T
  T A G H N C L T N S O H Y U A R B
  W H O H A I I A C O S E Q E A I P
  A P T E A M R L T K R Y N F C A R
  O M S E E N O D R I Z I O I C B E
  F O R E T S D A A A O K H K X E W
        O R E D D L R E R N R H O
        T R S E C O O D A S I
        N A P H R W W T A S E
```

Theme:_____

Answers on page 177.

Misleading Sequence

ANALYSIS   CREATIVE THINKING

In the progression below, circle 2 numbers that equal 18 when added together.

1   2   3   4   5   6   7   8   9

Missing Connections

LANGUAGE   PLANNING

It's a crossword without the clues! Use the letters below to fill in the empty spaces in the crossword grid. When you are finished, you'll have both words that read across and words that read down, crossword-style.

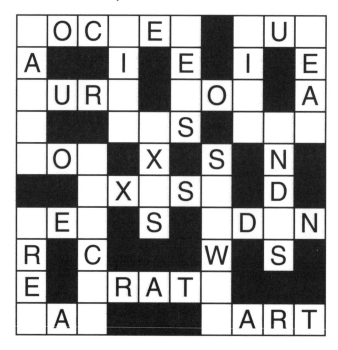

A A B C D E E E G H H I I K

L N N N P P P R T T T T W Y

Answers on page 177.

Sloop John B. and Co. (Part 1)

LANGUAGE **MEMORY**

This may be an easy cruise for nautical types. Look at the shipshape crossword for 2 minutes. Time yourself! Then turn the page, and see how many of these words you remember.

Sloop John B. and Co. (Part II)

LANGUAGE   **MEMORY**

(Don't read this until you've read the previous page!)

Check off the words you saw in the boat shape on page 67:

___ FRIGATE   ___ SUBMARINE

___ BARK   ___ HOUSEBOAT

___ DORY   ___ OUTRIGGER

___ BARGE   ___ FERRY

___ YACHT   ___ BRIGANTINE

___ SKIFF   ___ WHALER

___ YAWL   ___ SLOOP

___ CANOE   ___ JUNK

Toys

COMPUTATION   **LOGIC**

A father bought his 3 children 7 toys costing 25P, 27P, 30P, 41P, 58P, 87P, and 95P. Two children received toys totaling the same value. What was that value? What was the value of the toys each child received?

Answers on page 178.

Hidden Critters

The sentences below are crawling with hidden critters. Look carefully. Can you find an animal name in each sentence?

1. She epitomizes elegance. _____

2. Soap is anti-germ. _____

3. He made errors. _____

4. Urban renewal rushes on. _____

5. He did the task unknowingly. _____

6. Her badge revealed her mission. _____

7. I went to a dandy party. _____

8. Smell new olfactory sensations. _____

9. Would you rebuff a local swain? _____

10. Yes, if Roger will. _____

Trivia on the Brain

The part of the brain that stops a person from acting on inappropriate impulses is the orbitofrontal cortex, which is located at the front of the frontal lobes.

Answers on page 178.

Digital Sudoku

LOGIC

Fill in the grid with the numbers 1 through 6 so that each number appears once in each row, column, and 2×3 block. The numbers appear in digital form. Some segments have already been filled in for you.

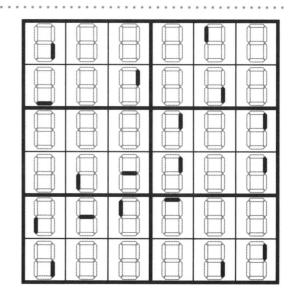

Fitting Words

LANGUAGE   LOGIC   PLANNING

In this miniature crossword, the clues are listed randomly and are numbered for convenience only. It is up to you to figure out the placement of the 9 answers. To help you out, we've already inserted one letter in the grid, and this is the only occurrence of that letter in the completed puzzle.

Clues

1. "Quiet!"
2. Heavy books
3. Domino on the piano
4. "Goodbye, Pierre!"
5. Golf supporters
6. Screen star
7. Foul matter
8. Spill clumsily
9. VIP's ride

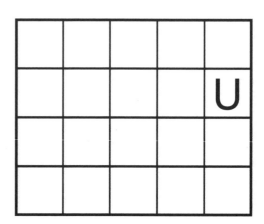

Answers on page 178.

Number Crossword

Fill in this crossword with numbers instead of letters. Use the clues to determine which of the numbers 1 through 9 belongs in each square. No zeros are used.

Across

1. A multiple of 21
3. Consecutive digits, descending
5. Consecutive even digits, in some order
6. A multiple of 23

Down

1. A perfect square
2. A perfect square
3. A perfect cube
4. Its middle digit is the sum of its 2 outside digits

Word Columns

Find the hidden phrase by using the letters directly below each of the blank squares. Each letter in a column is used only once in the squares above it.

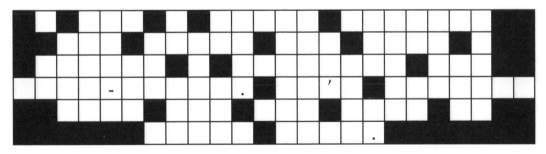

```
                        r  a
      h        y  c  e        a  a     i     a              p
   w  h  a  h  r  h  h  u  e     a  t     b  w  r  k  a  i  l
   I  o  f  g  p  t  i  o  e  f  o  d  n  y  s  a  c  m  a  u  n
   a  l  u  o  t  o  a  a  g  r  e  d  k  y  p  i  t  g  n  z  i
   h  b  t  g  e  t  t  e  s  r  c  I  t  l  s  f  h  e  f  o  r  n  g
```

Answers on page 178.

Rhyme Time

Answer each clue below with a pair of rhyming words. The numbers that follow each clue indicate how many letters are in each word. For example, "Azure African antelope (4, 3)" would be "blue gnu."

1. Azure African antelope (4, 3): _____

2. Farmer's trade (4, 4): _____

3. Skate that's away from its ilk (5, 3): _____

4. Zoo employee with a lower salary (7, 6): _____

5. A very small order of ribs (5, 4): _____

6. Single objective (4, 4): _____

7. Bovine that just ate (4, 4): _____

8. Tag on a fur coat (5, 5): _____

9. Tardier reptile (5, 5): _____

10. Summary of the full story (5, 6): _____

11. Late crop (6, 6): _____

12. Trumpeter's old instrument (4, 4): _____

13. An entire navy (8, 5): _____

14. Where is Lord Lucan?, for example (7, 7): _____

Answers on page 178.

Swimming with the Cubes

Only 1 of the cubes below matches the centre pattern exactly. Which is it?

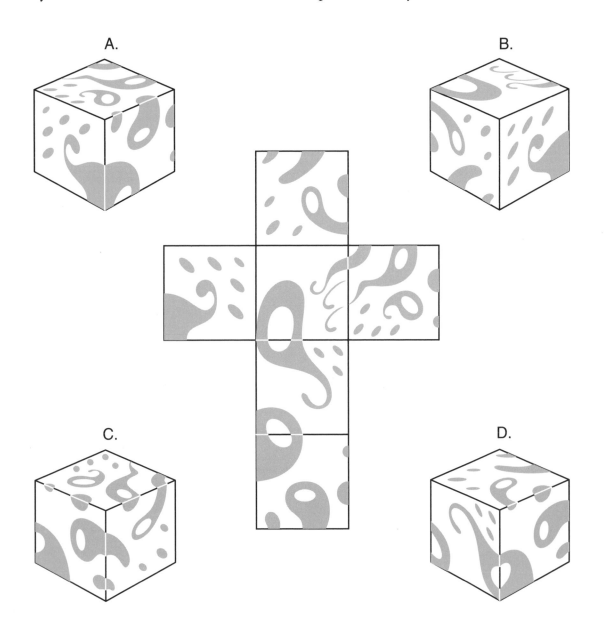

A.

B.

C.

D.

Answer on page 178.

Between the Lines

Solve for the middle (undefined) word in each set. All three words in each set would appear on the same page in the dictionary, in the order given. Then use the five middle words to complete the quote at the end of the puzzle.

Example: putter: *to work at random; tinker*

        puzzle

        pygmy: *small person of Africa*

1. a) __ h __ __ __: *adapted to cutting or piercing*

   b) __ __ __ __ __ __ __

   c) __ __ __ __ __ - e __ __ __: *having keen sight*

2. a) __ __ __ __ b __ __: *having qualities that attract affection*

   b) __ __ __ __

   c) __ __ __ __ __ __: *attractive; graceful*

3. a) __ r __ __ __ l __ __ __: *choose in advance*

   b) __ __ __ __ __ __ c __

   c) __ __ __ __ __ __ __: *gift*

4. a) a __ __ __ __ __ __: *to depart secretly and hide oneself*

   b) __ __ __ e __ __ __

   c) __ __ __ __ __ __ __: *not present*

5. a) __ t __ __ __ __ __ __: *capacity for exertion or endurance*

   b) __ __ __ __ __ g __ __ __ n

   c) __ __ __ __ __ __ __ __ u __: *vigorously active*

"_____ _____s _____, _____ _____s it."

—Thomas Fuller

Trivia on the Brain

You build your body up by exercising, such as lifting weights, running or walking, and swimming. Well, you also need to build your brain by exercising it and performing mental activities. So work puzzles, play board games, and do other stimulating mental activities to help prevent dementia and reduce memory loss. And have fun, too!

Answers on page 178.

Motel Hideout

A thief hides out in one of the 45 motel rooms listed in the chart below. The motel's in-house detective received a sheet of four clues, signed "The Holiday Thief." Using the clues below, the detective found the room number within 15 minutes—but by that time, the thief had fled. Can you find the thief faster?

1. Of the two digits in the room number, one of them is an odd number and the other is even.

2. The second digit in the room number is more than twice as large as the first digit.

3. The room number cannot be evenly divided by 7.

4. If the two digits in the room number exchanged positions, it would still be a room number in the motel as listed in the chart.

51	52	53	54	55	56	57	58	59
41	42	43	44	45	46	47	48	49
31	32	33	34	35	36	37	38	39
21	22	23	24	25	26	27	28	29
11	12	13	14	15	16	17	18	19

Answer on page 178.

Diagonal Switch

Can you find a single, unbroken path from the circle in the upper left corner to the circle in the lower right? If you move horizontally or vertically, you must move only to the same shape (for example, from a square to a square). You must change shapes when you move diagonally. You may not land on an empty square. There's only one way to complete the maze.

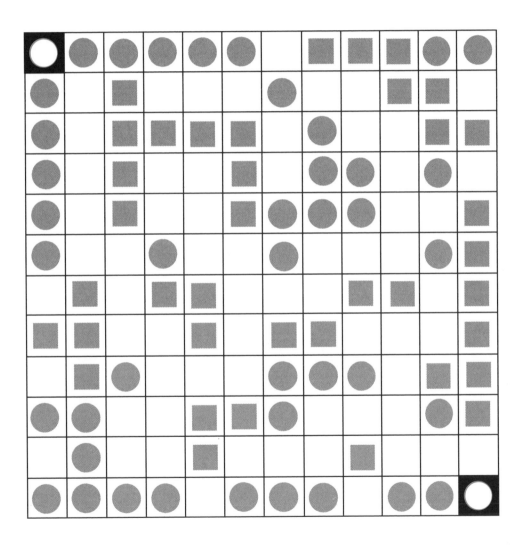

Answer on page 178.

Fitting Words

In this miniature crossword, the clues are listed randomly and are numbered for convenience only. It is up to you to figure out the placement of the 9 answers. To help you out, we've already inserted one letter in the grid, and this is the only occurrence of that letter in the completed puzzle.

Clues

1. Comedian's stock-in-trade
2. Suva's country
3. Recipe instruction
4. Element symbolized by Fe
5. Really angry
6. Exam
7. Clumsy
8. Collect leaves
9. Original

(grid with letter **P** inserted near the bottom row)

A Sign of the Times

COMPUTATION   LOGIC

Fill each square in the grid with a digit from 1 through 5. When the numbers in each row are multiplied, you should arrive at the total in the right-hand column. When the numbers in each column are multiplied, you should arrive at the total on the bottom line. The numbers in each corner-to-corner diagonal, when multiplied, must produce the totals in the upper and lower right corners, respectively.

Row totals (top to bottom): 40, 72, 40, 180, 25

Column totals (left to right): 36, 75, 80, 60, 300

Answers on page 179.

What's for Dinner?

There are 18 differences between the top and the bottom scenes of this family dinner. Can you find all of them?

Answers on page 179.

All the Colours of the Rainbow

Every word listed is contained within the group of letters on page 81. The words can be found in a straight line horizontally, vertically, or diagonally. They may read either backward or forward. Circle them, then determine what the leftover letters spell.

AMBER	GREEN	RED
AQUA	HAZEL	ROSE
AZURE	ICE	RUBY
BISTER	INDIGO	RUSSET
BLUE	IVORY	SCARLET
BUFF	LAVENDER	SILVER
CARMINE	MAGENTA	TAN
CHARTREUSE	MAROON	TANGERINE
CINNABAR	MAUVE	TURQUOISE
COPPER	MYRTLE	VERMILION
CREAM	NAVY	VIOLET
CRIMSON	ORANGE	WHITE
EMERALD	PEARL	WINE
FUCHSIA	PUCE	YELLOW
GRAY	PURPLE	

```
C R R E D N E V A L E R O S E
R R C D O N V R A A U Q A I N
E U I G I E U Y T M Y R T L E
P L E M E R A L D E I E N V L
P L R M S Z M N O N L W E E G
O A G A U O R O D E E R G R R
C T N R E E N I R E G N A T E
B E E O R P G L N W L Y M C T
U L G O T O A I E P H A I E S
E O I N R N W M U Z Y I S N I
C I N N A B A R B R A S T E B
N V D I H R P E O E U H G E L
M A E R C L O V O R R C V R U
I O V L E S I O U Q R U T G E
R U B Y E L L O W E T F F U B
```

Leftover letters spell:_____

Trivia on the Brain
The childhood years are the best time to
develop strong math, logic, and musical skills.

Answers on page 179.

Word Columns

Find the hidden phrase by using the letters directly below each of the blank squares.
Each letter in a column is used only once in the squares above it.

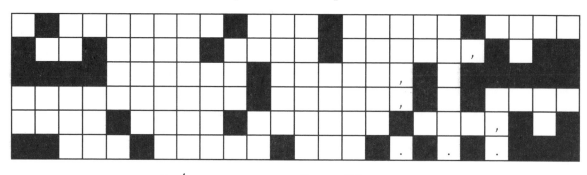

```
        e  t              r  w
   f    r  a  t  w  e     a  e     f  a        a
   u    a  l  l  o  v  s  n  f  a  i  a  k  s        y
f  o  c  e  r  i  e  n  e  t  r  l  t  o  e  s     l  u        a  a
I  o  m  e  f  g  i  u  s  r  h  o  r  n  e  v  e  r  s     d  a  l  p
g  a  b  n  d  a  r  i  o  t  s  g  a  n  d  d  l  o  a  t  b  r  o  l
```

Find the Booty!

Fill in the blanks below using the clues given; we've inserted a few letters to help out.
Then take the middle 3 letters of each word, put them all together, and rearrange them
to make a word that means "booty."

1. Amuse an audience: __ __ T __ __ __ __ I __

2. "And a cast of ___!": ___ H __ __ __ __ __ __ S

3. Major celeb: __ __ P __ __ __ T __ __

What you'd be glad to find: _____

Answers on page 179.

Overload of O's

Inside this picture is an overload of things beginning with the letter **O.** We count 11 things. How many can you find?

All Together Now

What letter completes this group of 4?

J,   P,   G,   _____

Answers on page 179.

Take 30

Alf was the 93rd caller to a radio-station contest and was told he would win a car if he could go into a room and come out exactly 30 minutes later. The room had no clock, and Alf was not allowed to wear a watch or bring in anything else that tells time. The only thing he could take into the room was a lighter and a candle in a candle holder (supplied by the radio station) that was guaranteed to burn completely in exactly one hour. Alf was not allowed to use a ruler to measure exactly halfway down the candle. Alf went into the room and emerged exactly 30 minutes later to win the car. How did he do it?

Scrambled Squares

LANGUAGE   PLANNING

Place the letters of the following words into the diagrams so that each horizontal row of letters spells a new word. The first words have been placed for you.

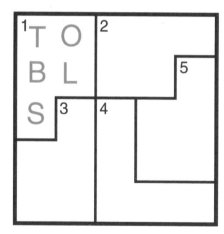
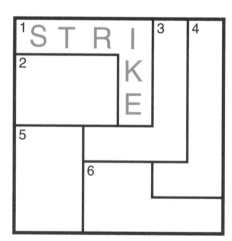

1. BOLTS	1. STRIKE
2. NAKED	2. ROBINS
3. AUNTS	3. REFERS
4. PAIRS	4. NETTER
5. ELAND	5. CAESAR
	6. PATTEN

Answers on page 179.

Car Chase

These people have had a great day shopping in the city! One problem: They can't find the parking garage to get their car. Can you help?

Answer on page 180.

Accelerate for Power

Times Squared

COMPUTATION   **LOGIC**

· ·

Fill each square in the grid with a digit from 1 through 8. When the numbers in each row are multiplied, you should arrive at the total in the right-hand column. When the numbers in each column are multiplied, you should arrive at the total on the bottom line. Important: You may place the number 1 only once in any row or column; other numbers can be repeated.

Hint: Some of the grid squares contain 5's and 7's. Identify those first.

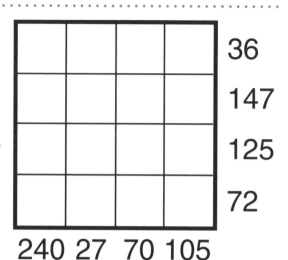

36
147
125
72

240 27 70 105

Letter Quilt

LOGIC

· ·

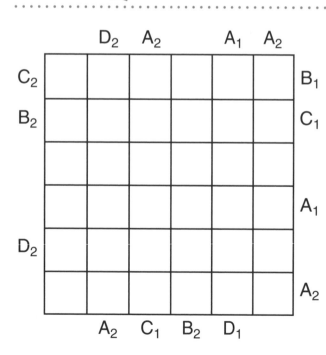

Each row and column contains A, B, C, D, and two empty squares. Each letter-and-number indicator refers to the first or second of the four letters encountered when reading inward. Can you complete the grid?

If you need a hint to get you started, see the bottom of the second column on page 190.

Answers on page 180.

Famous Address

LANGUAGE   PLANNING

Complete the horizontal phrase by finding the merging phrases.

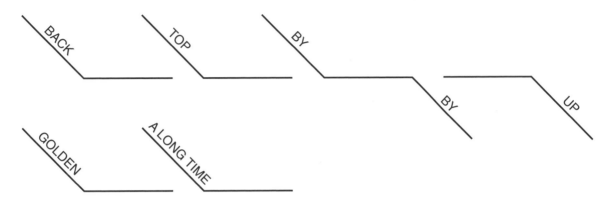

Word Ladders

LANGUAGE   PLANNING

Change just 1 letter on each line to go from the top word to the bottom word. Do not change the order of the letters. You must have a common English word at each step.

1. HAIR

————
————
————
————

CARE

2. CUP

————
————
————

TEA

Answers on page 180.

Mirror, Mirror

There's no trick here, only a challenge: Draw the mirror image of each of these familiar objects. You may find it harder than you think!

Unbearable Jigsaw

It's the national animal of Finland, and the adjective for it is *ursine*. These shapes, when fitted together properly, will give you its silhouette. The pieces haven't been flipped, rotated, or otherwise changed—all you have to do is fit them together with your eyes.

Answer on page 180.

Accelerate for Power

Planks Galore

COMPUTATION   LOGIC   SPATIAL REASONING

How many individual boards are in the cubes below? All boards are the same size, and all rows and columns run to completion (there are no half boards).

Logidoku

LOGIC

To solve the puzzle, place the numbers 1 through 8 only once in every row, column, long diagonal, irregular shape, and 2×4 grid. From the starters given, can you complete the puzzle?

	4					8	
		4					5
					3		
						7	
3		5		2			8
			6				

Answers on page 180.

ABCD

Every cell in the 6×6 grid contains one of 4 letters: A, B, C, or D. No letter can be horizontally or vertically adjacent to itself. The tables above and to the left of the grid indicate how many times each letter appears in that column or row. We've filled in 2 of the cells to get you started.

Can you complete the grid?

A	0	1	3	1	2	2
B	2	1	1	2	2	1
C	2	3	1	1	0	2
A B C D	2	1	1	2	2	1

A	B	C	D						
1	2	2	1						C
1	2	2	1			D			
2	1	1	2						
1	1	2	2						
1	1	2	2						
3	2	0	1						

Let Freedom Ring

Reveal the horizontal phrase by completing the merging phrases.

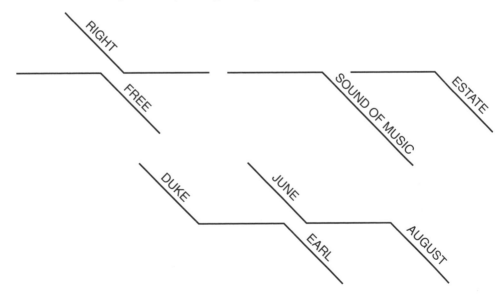

RIGHT
FREE
DUKE
JUNE
EARL
SOUND OF MUSIC
AUGUST
ESTATE

Answers on page 180.

Accelerate for Power

Cube Fold

Which of the 12 figures below would not form a perfect cube if it were folded along the dotted lines?

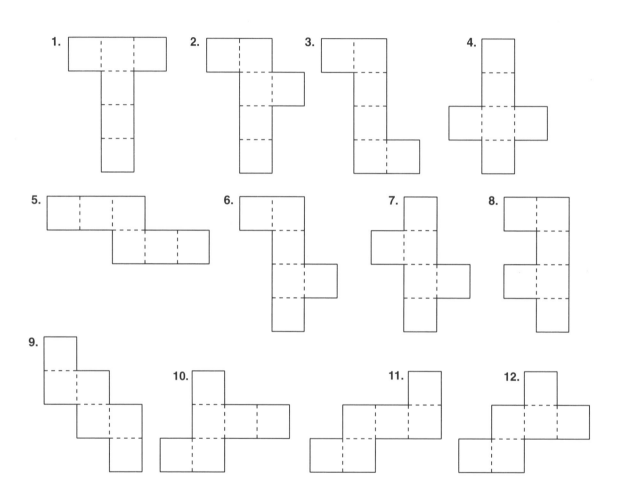

Trivia on the Brain

The consistency of a brain is very much like warm butter!

Answer on page 180.

Cross Count

Each number you land on in this maze tells you how many squares away either vertically or horizontally your next move must be. You may not move diagonally. For example, your first move from the 4 in the upper left corner must be either 4 squares vertically (to the 2) or 4 squares horizontally (to the 3). If you land on a square with a zero, you've reached a dead end and will need to backtrack. There's only one way to reach the star.

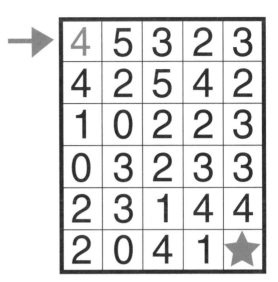

Cast-a-word

There are 4 dice, the faces of which have different letters of the alphabet. Random throws of the dice produced the words in this list. Can you figure out which letters appear on the 6 faces of each dice?

BUSY	CLUE	FLIP	JACK	PRAY
CANE	DAUB	GLUT	KILT	QUAD
CLIP	EXIT	HOME	MEAD	ZONE

Answers on page 181.

Quilt Quest

ATTENTION

VISUAL SEARCH

The small tricoloured pattern below appears exactly 3 times in the quilt at right. Find all 3 instances. Note that the pattern might appear rotated but not overlapped and/or mirrored in the quilt.

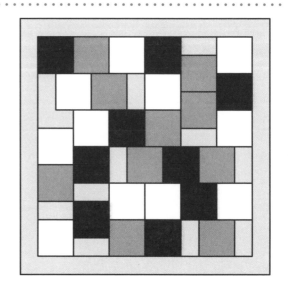

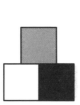

Word Jigsaw

LANGUAGE

SPATIAL PLANNING

Fit the pieces into the frame to form words reading across and down crossword-style. There is no need to rotate any of the pieces; they will fit as shown, with each piece used exactly once.

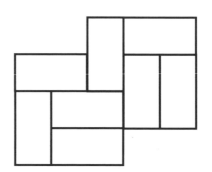

Answers on page 181.

Fun with Numbers

COMPUTATION   LOGIC

What 3-digit number can be divided by 3, have the order of the digits in the resulting number reversed, have 1 subtracted from that reversed number, and yet end up being unchanged?

Famous Last Line

LANGUAGE   SPATIAL PLANNING

Rearrange the tiles to produce an immortal last line from the film "Casablanca." Hint: One of the characters is named Blaine.

INN	ING	BEA	THI	S I	A	IS,
NK	IEN	LOU	I	OF	UTI	FR
S T	THI	DSH	IP.	HE	BEG	FUL

Trivia on the Brain

The brain and a computer are very similar. Both adapt and learn, but the brain is much faster and better at learning new things. A computer, on the other hand, can perform many complex tasks simultaneously. The brain is not as good at multitasking. It is very difficult for most people to recite a poem and perform a division problem in their head at the same time. But the autonomic nervous system of the brain does control breathing, heart rate, and blood pressure at the same time other brain areas perform various mental tasks.

Answers on page 181.

Star Power

To complete the puzzle, place digits in the grid so that each star is surrounded by every digit from 1 through 8 with no repeats.

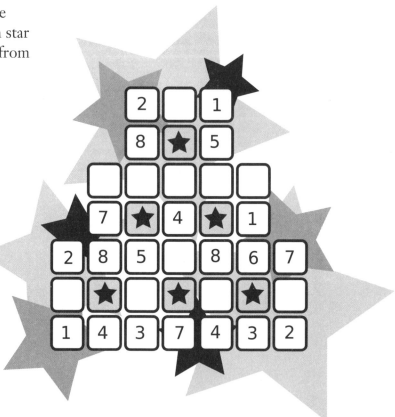

Vocal Vowels

LANGUAGE

All vowels of this word are given in the correct order below. Find this word that may define a South American person or culture.

A E I E A

Answers on page 181.

Word Jigsaw

Fit the pieces into the frame to form words reading across and down crossword-style. There is no need to rotate any of the pieces; they will fit as shown, with each piece used exactly once.

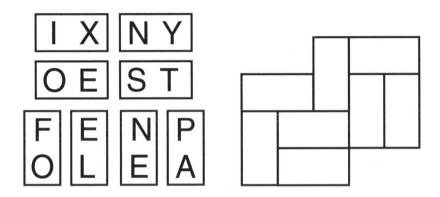

Face the Blocks

All 12 blocks in the illustration are the same size and shape. Count how many times each block touches the side, or face, of another block. Blocks that connect only at the corners or edges do not count.

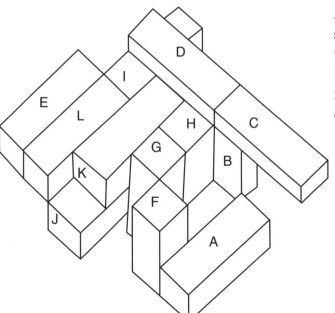

A __   E __   I __

B __   F __   J __

C __   G __   K __

D __   H __   L __

Answers on page 181.

Red, White, and Blue

Each row, column, and corner-to-corner diagonal contains 2 reds, 2 whites, and 2 blues. From the clues given, can you complete the grid?

1. The blues are adjacent.
2. One white is between 2 reds and the other is between 2 blues.
3. The blues are somewhere to the right of the rightmost red.
4. The whites are adjacent.
5. The blues are adjacent and bounded by the whites.
6. The whites are adjacent and bounded by the reds.

A. One of the reds is bounded by 2 whites.
B. The blues are adjacent and bounded by the reds.
C. There are no adjacent squares of the same color.
D. The reds are adjacent and bounded by the blues.
E. The reds are adjacent.
F. The pattern of the first 3 cells is repeated in the second 3.

	A	B	C	D	E	F
1						
2						
3						
4						
5						
6						

Answers on page 181.

Cast-a-word

LOGIC · PROBLEM SOLVING

There are 4 dice, the faces of which have different letters of the alphabet. Random throws of the dice produced the words in the list below. Can you figure out which letters appear on the 6 faces of each dice?

BONY	DROP	HARE	PONY	TURN
CHIT	FLAB	JOKE	QUIP	WEAR
COVE	GRIM	MOCK	SOAR	WIFE

Word Columns

LANGUAGE · PLANNING · SPATIAL REASONING

Find the hidden phrase by using the letters directly below each of the blank squares. Each letter in a column is used only once in the squares above it.

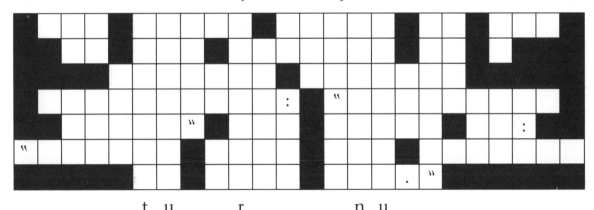

Answers on page 182.

FULL SPEED AHEAD

Last Laugh Department

LANGUAGE   LOGIC

What makes a bestseller? How publishers wish they knew. Below, you'll find six cryptographically disguised reasons why a writer should never give up. But you'll have to break the code first! The code is the same for each cryptogram.

Hint: Look for repeated letters. **E, T, A, O, N, R,** and **I** are the most often used letters. A single letter is usually **A** or **I;** OF, IS, and IT are common 2-letter words; THE and AND are common 3-letter words.

1. XZXFJX UJBOWFOS'W GOBWF TVVR,

   FJS PEWFSBOVMW XGGXOB XF WFENSW,

   DJOUJ OKFBVHMUSH JSB TSNZOXK

   HSFSUFOYS JSBUMNS LVOBVF, DXW

   BSQSUFSH TE FJS GOBWF WOC

   LMTNOWJSBW WJS WMTP<u>O</u>FFSH <u>O</u>F FV.

2. QVJK ZBOWJXP'W GOBWF KVYSN, *X*

   FOPS FV RONN, DXW BSQSUFSH TE

   FDSKFE-SOZJF LMTNOWJSBW.

3. BVTSBF D. LOBWOZ'W *ISK XKH FJS XBF*

   VG PVFVBUEUNS PXOKFSKXKUS DXW

   BSQSUFSH—VMUJ!—VKS JMKHBSH XKH

FDSKFE-VKS FOPSW TSGVBS OF TSUXPS X TSWFWSNNSB GVB PVBBVD OK KOKSFSSK WSYSKFE-GVMB.

4. XEK BXKH'W *FJS GVMKFXOKJSXH* DXW BSQSUFSH TE FJS GOBWF FDSNYS LMTNOWJSBW WJS XLLBVXUJSH.

5. Q. R. BVDNOKZ'W GOBWF TVVR, *JXBBE LVFFSB XKH FJS LJONVWVLJSB'W WFVKS,* DXW FMBKSH HVDK TE KOKS LMT-NOWJSBW, OKUNMHOKZ JXBLSB-UVNNOKW XKH LSKZMOK, TSGVBS TNVVPWTMBE WOZKSH OF ML.

6. HB. WSMWW'W GOBWF UJONHBSK'W TVVR, *XKH FV FJOKR FJXF O WXD OF VK PMNTSBBE WFBSSF,* DXW BSQSUFSH TE FDSKFE-WOC LMTNOWJSBW TSGVBS OF DXW LMTNOWJSH OK KOKSFSSK FJOBFE-WSYSK.

Answers on page 182.

Merit Badge

Biff the brand-new Boy Scout wants to get a merit badge for going on a long hike. It's an 8-day hike, and he wants to be prepared because he heard somewhere that this is the Scouts' motto. Biff knows that even the biggest and best Scout can only carry enough food and water for a 5-day hike. He also knows he'll be disqualified if he uses an animal to carry extra food and water for him. On the other hand, Biff knows he may bring other Scouts with him as food carriers to help him finish the hike. What is the least number of Scouts Biff will need to bring along in order for him to complete the 8-day hike safely?

Logidoku

LOGIC

Use deductive logic to complete the grid so that each row, column, corner-to-corner diagonal, irregular shape, and 3×3 box contains the numbers 1 through 9 in some order. The solution is unique.

6		9						
	1		7		6		5
	2						
3				8			2
					4		
		5					9
				7			
4							3

Answers on page 182.

Roman Numerals Challenge COMPUTATION LOGIC

This is more difficult than it sounds, but give it a try—it's fun! Write the number for 99,989 in Roman numerals. Note: A line over a number (or numbers) in Roman numerals indicates that the number is multiplied by 1,000.

$$I = 1 \qquad \overline{X} = 10,000$$
$$V = 5 \qquad \overline{C} = 100,000$$
$$X = 10 \qquad \overline{M} = 1,000,000$$
$$L = 50$$
$$C = 100$$
$$D = 500$$
$$M = 1,000$$

Fitting Words LANGUAGE LOGIC PLANNING

In this miniature crossword, the clues are listed randomly and are numbered for convenience only. It is up to you to figure out the placement of the nine answers. To help you out, we've already inserted one letter in the grid, and this is the only occurrence of that letter in the completed puzzle.

Clues

1. Flung
2. Flung
3. Foot part
4. Consumer
5. Bad lighting?
6. Was in on
7. Public fight
8. Seal in one's bathroom
9. Solitary

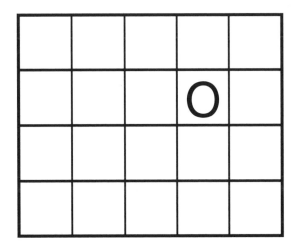

Answers on page 182.

My Kind of Town

LANGUAGE

ATTENTION   VISUAL SEARCH

Every word listed below is contained within the group of letters on the next page. The words can be found in a straight line horizontally, vertically, or diagonally. They may read either backward or forward.

As an added challenge, see if you can figure out the theme of this puzzle.

ALIVE AGAIN

ALL I CARE ABOUT

ALL THAT JAZZ

BEGINNINGS

CALL ON ME

CELL BLOCK TANGO

CHASIN' THE WIND

FUNNY HONEY

I CAN'T DO IT ALONE

I'M A MAN

I MOVE ON

JUST YOU 'N' ME

LOOK AWAY

MAKE ME SMILE

NOWADAYS

OLD DAYS

QUESTIONS 67 & 68

RAZZLE DAZZLE

ROXIE

25 OR 6 TO 4

YOU'RE NOT ALONE

Trivia on the Brain
The right and left hemispheres of your brain are connected by 50 million neurons.

```
    S  O  N  E  I  X  O  R  E  G  T  S  O
 P  E  R  E  M  L  Y  F  M  O  U  R  G  M  E
 D  C  I  N  A  N  A  Z  N  C  O  T  N  H  Q  E  I
 M  O  H  M  V  W  O  U  Z  B  A  A  I  U  E  C  C
 H  I  A  A  A  C  O  L  A  A  T  L  E  A  A  G  O
 N  N  A  K  S  Y  Y  E  A  K  D  S  L  N  N  D  S
 O  I  O  B  T  I  R  E  C  T  T  E  T  O  Z  N  M
 G  O  A  S  E  A  N  O  N  I  O  D  L  Z  N  A  S
 L  N  U  G  C  G  L  T  O  O  N  A  Z  K  M  R
 I  J  O  I  A  B  I  N  H  I  H  J  E  E  Z  4  E
 E  M  L  W  L  E  S  N  T  E  T  Y  M  R  O  A  O
 C  L  O  L  A  6  V  A  N  A  W  E  N  T  U  L  R
 A  O  E  V  7  D  L  I  H  I  S  I  6  N  D  O  R
 D  C  E  &  E  O  A  T  L  M  N  R  N  D  U  D  Y
 B  Y  6  T  N  O  L  Y  I  A  O  G  A  D  H  F  E
    8  R  E  O  L  N  L  S  5  C  Y  S  K  B  A
    N  D  A  C  E  H  2  I  S  C  A  G  O
```

Theme:_____

Answers on page 183.

Rhyme Time

Answer each clue below with a pair of rhyming words. The numbers that follow each clue indicate how many letters are in each word. For example, "Unexpected cash (5, 5)" would be "found pound."

1. Unexpected cash (5, 5): _____

2. Not the second batch of buffalo (5, 4): _____

3. Retaliate (6, 4): _____

4. Hubby's cue to new-fan wife (5, 4): _____

5. Surprise occurrence in a card game (5, 5): _____

6. The cheapest of jewelry (6, 4): _____

7. Office supply ready for the archives (5, 6): _____

8. Weathered poultry snack (6, 5): _____

9. Senior construction worker (5, 6): _____

10. Trendy flick (6, 5): _____

11. She was awarded a free meal (6, 6): _____

12. Roam far and wide (6, 6): _____

13. It withstands the strongest shocks (7, 6): _____

14. He runs on icy streets (6, 8): _____

15. Chocolate sweet clash (7, 7): _____

16. Pugilist with a weight handicap (7, 7): _____

17. No flat fish this (7, 8): _____

18. The entire army ran away (8, 7): _____

Answers on page 183.

Logidoku

Use deductive logic to complete the grid so that each row, column, corner-to-corner diagonal, irregular shape, and 3×3 box contains the numbers 1 through 9 in some order. The solution is unique.

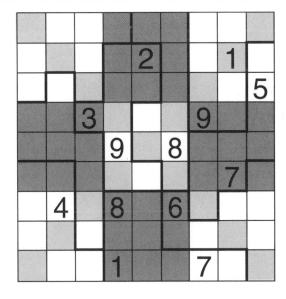

Word Jigsaw

Fit the pieces into the frame to form words reading across and down crossword-style. There is no need to rotate any of the pieces; they will fit as shown, with each piece used exactly once.

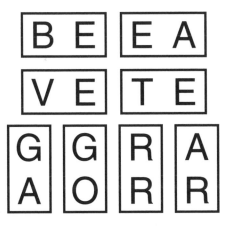

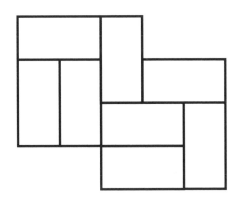

Answers on page 183.

Counting Up

ANALYSIS   CREATIVE THINKING

What is the next number in this common progression? What do these numbers represent?

$$1, 5, 10, 20, \underline{\quad\quad}$$

Geometric Shapes

LOGIC   SPATIAL REASONING

Divide the grid into smaller geometric shapes by drawing straight lines following either the full grid lines or the full diagonals of the square cells. Each formed shape must have exactly one symbol inside, which represents it but might not look identical to it. (In other words, a triangle you draw must have only a triangle symbol within it, although the drawn triangle and the triangle symbol may look slightly different.) Hints: The rectangle symbol cannot be contained in a square. The parallelogram is not inside a rectangle or square. Each trapezoid has two sides parallel, but its other two sides are not parallel.

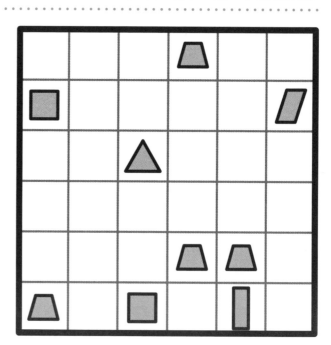

Trivia on the Brain

The fuel your brain uses to keep you moving and functioning is glucose, which comes from the carbohydrates you eat.

Answers on page 183.

Number-Crossed

Fill in this crossword with numbers instead of letters. Use the clues to determine which of the numbers 1 through 9 belongs in each square. No zeros are used.

Across

1. The 2 outside digits add up to the middle digit
4. A number with the pattern AABCC
6. A square
7. A multiple of 19
8. The sum of the first 2 digits is equal to the sum of the last 3 digits
10. A square

Down

1. Consecutive digits, ascending
2. A multiple of 13
3. Consecutive digits, descending
4. A cube
5. A square palindrome
9. A multiple of 17

Answers on page 183.

Flower Shop

Can you find things that have changed from the top picture to the bottom picture? We count 21 differences.

Answers on page 183.

Jigstars

These 12 jigsaw pieces can be put together to form 6 perfect 6-pointed stars. Using only your eyes, match up the correct pieces.

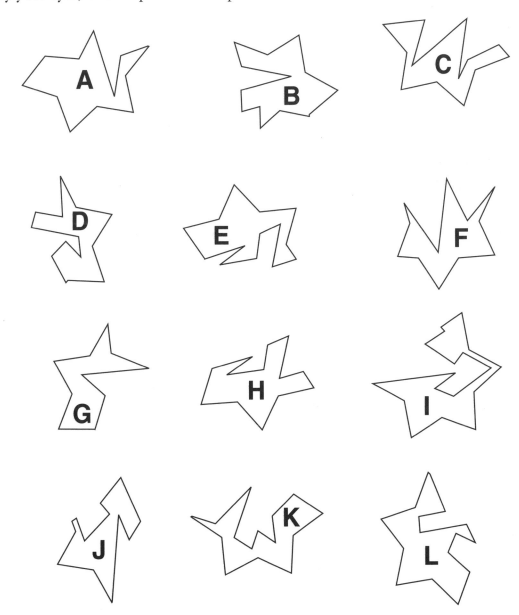

Answers on page 183.

Four Sisters

Upon her return from living abroad, Alberta, the youngest of 4 sisters, announced her shipboard marriage. Her 3 sisters, Carla, Paula, and Roberta were amazed by her husband's name. With the aid of the clues below, determine Alberta's husband's first and last names, as well as Carla's, Paula's, and Roberta's husbands' first and last names. The 4 men are Albert, Carl, Paul, and Robert. Their last names are Albertson, Carlson, Paulson, and Robertson.

1. No woman's husband has a first name that consists of her first name without the final "a"; no woman's last name consists of her first name without the final "a" and with "son" on the end; and no man's last name consists of his first name with "son" added at the end.

2. Paul is not married to Roberta, and Robert is not married to Paula.

3. No husband and wife have "bert" in both of their first names, but there is a man who has "bert" in his first and last names.

4. Carl's last name is not Paulson.

	ALBERT	CARL	PAUL	ROBERT	ALBERTSON	CARLSON	PAULSON	ROBERTSON
ALBERTA								
CARLA								
PAULA								
ROBERTA								
ALBERTSON								
CARLSON								
PAULSON								
ROBERTSON								

Answers on page 184.

Crisscross Puzzle

LANGUAGE · PLANNING · SPATIAL REASONING

Place the words below into this crossword.

3 Letters

cat
day
ice
sad
tab
via
van

4 Letters

nose
shot

5 Letters

catch
rabid
steam
takes

6 Letters

borrow
bought
clocks
global
motion
naming
repair

squash

7 Letters

arrived
barrier

8 Letters

brightly
restarts
upstairs

10 Letters

outrageous
roundabout

11 Letters

transaction

Answers on page 184.

Fair Freddy's Fondue Fete   COMPUTATION   LOGIC

Fair Freddy prides himself on always being fair. When Fair Freddy hosts one of his famous fondue parties, he diligently counts ahead of time to make sure everyone attending will get an equal number of bread cubes, not including Freddy, who has to watch his cholesterol. Fair Freddy invited Faye and Frank Franklin and their family for fondue. Faye replied, saying that depending on how much pain their babysitter can stand, the attendees might be just Faye and Frank, but they may be Faye, Frank, and baby Ford; or they could be Faye, Frank, baby Ford, and the quadruplets: Fee, Fy, Fo, and Fum. For Fair Freddy to be fair and have an equal number of bread cubes for each guest no matter which combination arrives, what is the minimum number he needs to cut up?

Times Squared   COMPUTATION   LOGIC

Fill in each empty square in the grid with a number from 1 through 5. When the numbers in each row are multiplied, you should arrive at the total in the right-hand column. When the numbers in each column are multiplied, you should arrive at the total on the bottom line. When the numbers in each of the two corner-to-corner diagonals are multiplied, you should arrive at the totals in the upper and lower right corners, respectively.

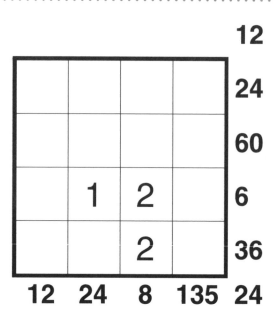

Answers on page 184.

Word Ladders

LANGUAGE   PLANNING

Change just one letter on each line to go from the top word to the bottom word. Do not change the order of the letters. You must have a common English word at each step.

1. CORN

   _____

   _____ shorebird

   _____

   _____

   _____ hot drinks

   PEAS

2. PRAYER

   _____ donkey

   _____

   _____

   _____

   HEAVEN

You Can't Have a Slice of This . . .

ANALYSIS   CREATIVE THINKING

Can you determine the next letter in this progression?

T. O, F, O, F, ___

Answers on page 184.

Classic Lit

Cryptograms are messages in substitution code. Break the code to read the message. For example, THE SMART CAT might become FVO QWGDF JGF if **F** is substituted for **T, V** for **H, O** for **E,** and so on.

Hint: Look for repeated letters. **E, T, A, O, N, R,** and **I** are the most often used letters. A single letter is usually **A** or **I;** OF, IS, and IT are common 2-letter words; THE and AND are common 3-letter words.

"FC FT M CHYCR YAFLIHTMZZB

MWJAPQZISUIS, CRMC M TFAUZI

KMA FA EPTTITTFPA PX M UPPS

XPHCYAI, KYTC DI FA QMAC PX

M QFXI."

—NMAI MYTCIA,

EHFSI MAS EHINYSFWI

Answer on page 184.

Fitting Words

In this miniature crossword, the clues are listed randomly and are numbered for convenience only. It is up to you to figure out the placement of the 9 answers. To help you out, we've already inserted one letter in the grid, and this is the only occurrence of that letter in the completed puzzle.

Clues

1. Refer to
2. Burn treatment
3. Excuse
4. Fountain order
5. Fountain request?
6. Yoga position
7. Colorful parrot
8. Choppers
9. Neighbour

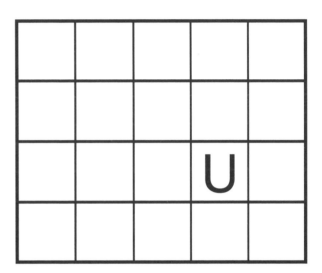

Trivia on the Brain

Your brain is 85 percent water. So getting dehydrated can have some bad effects on your brain, including a decrease in your ability to concentrate. Be sure to drink 8 glasses of water a day to stay healthy and alert.

Answers on page 184.

Full Speed Ahead

Letter Quilt

LOGIC

Each row and column contains A, B, C, D, and two blank squares. Each letter-and-number indicator refers to the first or second of the four letters encountered when travelling inward. Can you complete the grid?

If you need a hint to get you started, see the bottom of the second column on page 190.

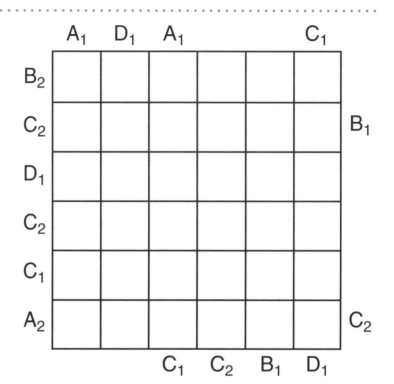

X × IV

COMPUTATION   LOGIC

The button in the equation stands for the multiplication sign. Notice that X multiplied by IV is not VII (since 10×4 does not equal 7). Leaving the button in its current posi-

tion, move 3 matchsticks to another position to make the equation correct. The button must still represent the multiplication sign, and the final equation must retain a sign of equality in it. Neither damaging nor overlapping of matchsticks is allowed.

Answers on page 184.

W-Cubed Rectangles

Use your eyes to determine which of the 4 patterns below can be folded to form the cube at the centre. No faces may be overlapped when forming the cube.

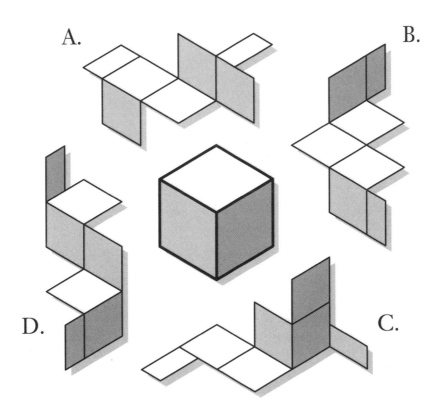

Trivia on the Brain

It's commonly thought that you use only 10 percent of your brain. Not so! You may not use every neuron in your brain at the same time, but each one is important.

Answers on page 184.

Star Power

To complete the puzzle, place numbers in the empty squares so that each star is surrounded by digits 1 through 8 with no repeats.

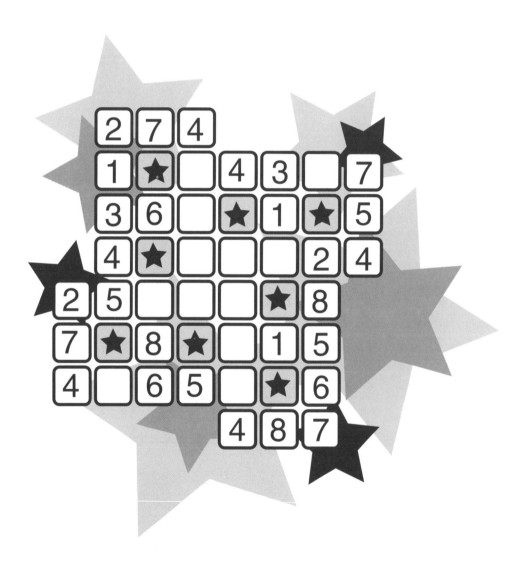

Answers on page 185.

Plus and Minuses

COMPUTATION   LOGIC

Put 1 plus sign (+) and 2 minus signs (–) between the digits below to create an equation that totals 100. Hint: You will need to combine some numbers to form multidigit numbers, but you may not rearrange the order of the numbers.

1   2   3   4   5   6   7   8   9 = 100

Circles and Numbers

COMPUTATION   LOGIC

Study the circles and numbers. What number should be substituted for the question mark?

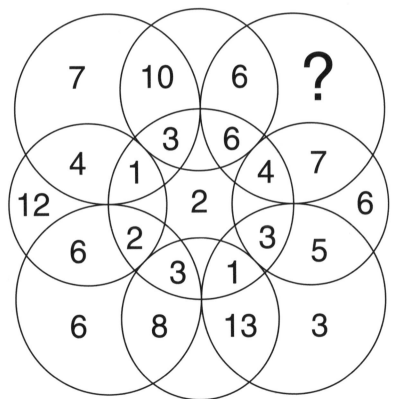

Answers on page 185.

A Four-midable Maze

COMPUTATION   PLANNING

The object of this puzzle is to form a path from the "4" diamond on the left to the "4" diamond on the right. Move only through diamonds containing multiples of 4, and move only through diamonds connected by a line.

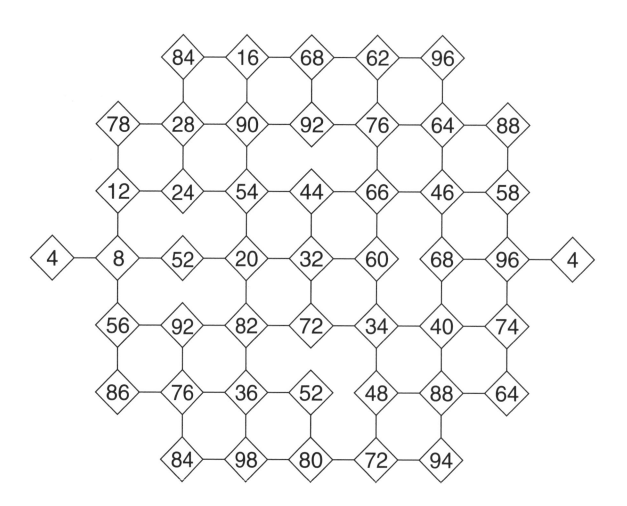

Answer on page 185.

Three for Two

That is, 3 letters for each of 2 answers!

Here's how it works: We provide 3 letters and a category, and you come up with 2 words from that category in which the 3 letters appear in the order shown. For example, if the category is "Signs of the Zodiac" and the 3-letter sequence given is **COR,** the answers would be **S**COR**PIO** and CAPRI**COR**N. If the 3-letter sequence given were **ARI** instead, the correct answers would be any 2 of the signs AQU**ARI**US, SAGITT**ARI**US, and **ARI**ES.

Letters	Category	
1. CAR	Food	_____
2. ERI	Great Lakes	_____
3. MBE	Months	_____
4. HAR	Deserts	_____
5. GAR	European Countries	_____

Trivia on the Brain
Consciousness emerges from the frontal lobes of your brain.

Answers on page 185.

Mirror, Mirror

There's no trick here, only a challenge: Draw the mirror image of each of these familiar objects. You may find it harder than you think!

M Is for Mystery

An anagram is a word or phrase made up of the rearranged letters of another word or phrase. Fill in the blanks in the conversation below by solving the anagrams (in capital letters) preceding them.

MERELY NEAT, AND TOM SAWYER—or, translated from the anagram, "Elementary, My Dear Watson!"

The great detective Shellshock Rome had settled himself into a comfortable leather armchair in Raffles, his gentlemen's club. Across from him, on the other side of a chessboard, sat his loyal companion, Two-Star Condo. Rome puffed slowly on his calabash, his slender fingers cradling the polished meerschaum bowl that looked like carved ivory but was, in fact, fashioned from a hard white clay. Condo, with white, moved pawn to e4. Rome smiled, knowing that his old friend could rarely resist the Ruy Lopez, a popular Spanish opening in chess.

"Cultural literacy is in decline, Condo," said Rome. "Hardly any of this generation has seen MAN OF STEEL CHALET _____ —Bogart, Lorre, Greenstreet!—much less read the book. I suppose HAG AT CHARITIES _____ _____ is the most successful female mystery author, since she has been outsold only by the Bible and Shakespeare! I rather enjoy her pleasant mysteries featuring OUR HELICOPTER _____, though those British cozies with SIMPLE ARMS _____ never quite caught my fancy. I do like Dorothy Sayers's creation, MY SPIDERWORT EEL _____, a scholar and a gentleman."

"What about GUINEA DUSTUP _____, Rome?" asked Condo. "Surely you can't dismiss GLAD AEROPLANE _____!" As expected, Condo's second move was king's knight to f3.

"I'd just as soon watch CHILEAN ARCH _____," sniffed Rome.

Answers on page 185.

Wacky Wordy

CREATIVE THINKING   **LANGUAGE**

Can you "read" the phrase below?

THEBRAIN DRAWING

It's a Song

LANGUAGE   **PLANNING**

Complete the horizontal phrases by finding the merging phrases.

WHAT

PIN

ON ONE

SHINING

,

PLY

PETE'S SAKE

MAIN EVENT

GIRLS

Answers on page 185.

Geometric Shapes

Divide the grid into smaller geometric shapes by drawing straight lines following either the full grid lines or the full diagonals of the square cells. Each formed shape must have exactly one symbol inside, which represents it but might not look identical to it. (In other words, a triangle you draw must have only a triangle symbol within it, although the drawn triangle and the triangle symbol may look slightly different.) Hints: The rectangle symbol cannot be contained in a square. Each trapezoid has two sides parallel, but its other two sides are not parallel.

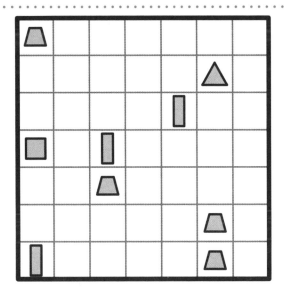

Word Jigsaw

Fit the pieces into the frame to form words reading across and down crossword-style. There is no need to rotate any of the pieces; they will fit as shown, with each piece used exactly once.

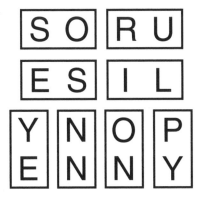
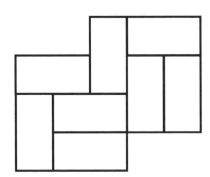

Answers on page 185.

Star Power

To complete the puzzle, place numbers in the empty squares so that each star is surrounded by digits 1 through 8 with no repeats.

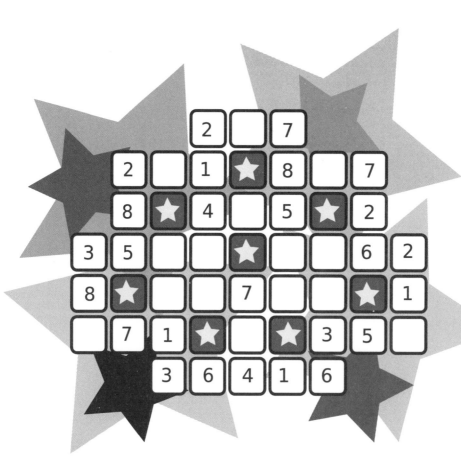

Trivia on the Brain

Your brain is constantly monitoring and fine-tuning what is going on in your body—24 hours a day, year after year—without you even being aware of it.

Answers on page 185.

Around Five Cubes

Three lines wind around the trio of 5-cube groups in the illustration below. Each line is a closed loop. Determine which 2 of these loops have exactly the same pattern. They are not mirrored.

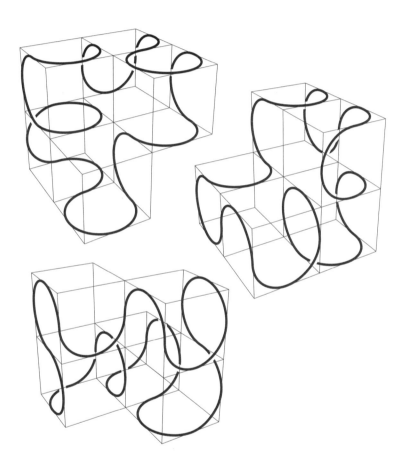

Trivia on the Brain
Calcium, as we know, is good for bone health, but it is also needed for nerve-impulse conduction throughout the body.

Answer on page 186.

Diagonal Jump

Can you find a single, unbroken path from the circle in the upper left corner to the circle in the lower right? Your path must move diagonally from circle to circle, with one twist—you can jump over any 1 diamond, as long as there is a circle on the opposite side of it. There's only one way to complete the maze.

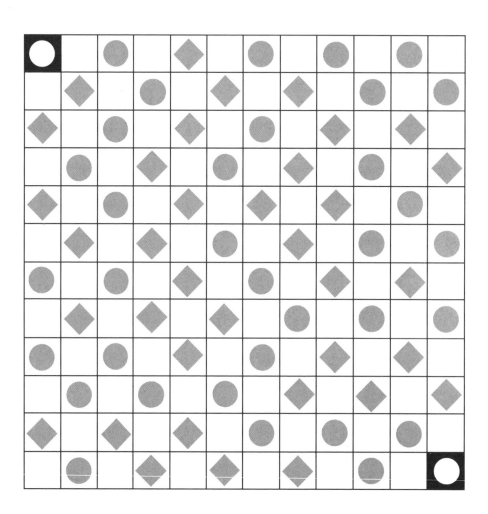

Answer on page 186.

Geometric Shapes

Divide the grid into smaller geometric shapes by drawing straight lines following either the full grid lines or the full diagonals of the square cells. Each formed shape must have exactly one symbol inside, which represents it but might not look identical to it. (In other words, a triangle you draw must have only a triangle symbol within it, although the drawn triangle and the triangle symbol may look slightly different.) Hints: The rectangle symbol cannot be contained in a square. Each trapezoid has two sides parallel, but its other two sides are not parallel.

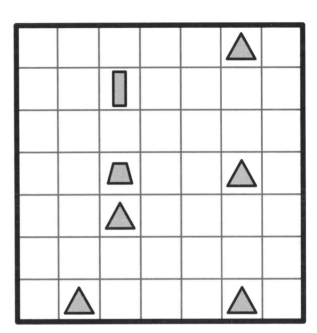

Trivia on the Brain

You don't have to accept the effects of aging on your brain—you can develop your brain throughout life. In addition to puzzling, getting physical exercise, eating well, maintaining social ties, and engaging in an enjoyable hobby are good for the brain.

Answer on page 186.

Shoe Sale

The shoe sale is over, and now the salesman needs to match up the 21 remaining pairs. Can you help him out? And can you spot the shoe that has no mate?

Answers on page 186.

Cross Count

COMPUTATION   LANGUAGE   PLANNING

In the chart below, all the letters of the alphabet have been given a value. Use the chart to fill in the squares to create 4-letter words that add up to the numbers beside the rows and below the columns.

1	2	3	4	5	6	7	8	9
A	B	C	D	E	F	G	H	I
J	K	L	M	N	O	P	Q	R
S	T	U	V	W	X	Y	Z	

R		B		22
			L	21
	E		[1]	9
	[9] E		[5]	21
17	24	18	14	

Coffee Break

LOGIC   PROBLEM SOLVING

There are 2 empty coffee cafetieres. One holds 3 cups, and the other holds 5 cups. There is also an unlimited supply of hot water and a packet of coffee that, when added to 1 cup of water, produces a coffee concentration of 100 percent. Using only these supplies, how would you make 5 cups of coffee that have a concentration of 12 percent?

Trivia on the Brain

Raw nuts and seeds supply essential fatty acids your brain needs to function. Walnuts especially are loaded with these healthy oils. Other foods that contain them include pumpkin seeds and flax seeds.

Answers on page 186.

Road Trip!

Can you help this family on holiday make it from southern California all the way to Maine?

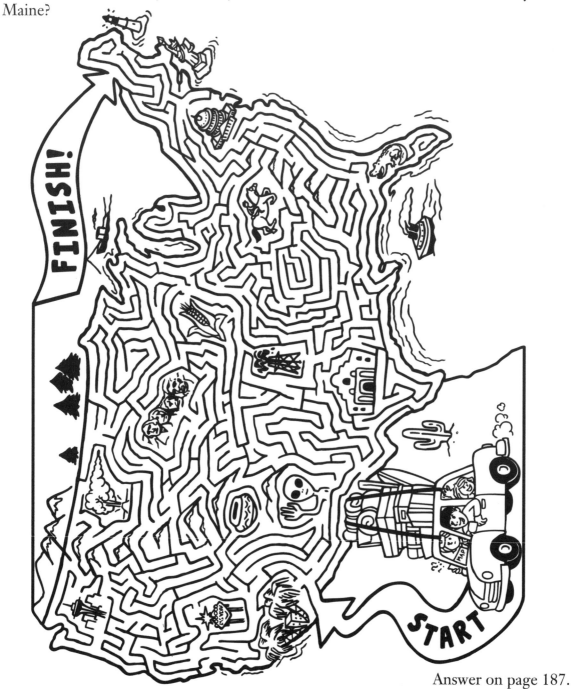

Answer on page 187.

Odd-Even Logidoku

Use deductive logic to complete the grid so that each row, column, corner-to-corner diagonal, irregular shape, and 3×3 box contains the numbers 1 through 9 in some order. You may only place even numbers in boxes with the letter E. The solution is unique.

Quilt Quest

The small tricoloured pattern below appears exactly 3 times in the quilt at left. Find all 3 instances. Note that the pattern may appear rotated but not overlapped and/or mirrored in the quilt.

Answers on page 187.

Star Power

To complete the puzzle, place numbers in the empty squares so that each star is surrounded by digits 1 through 8 with no repeats.

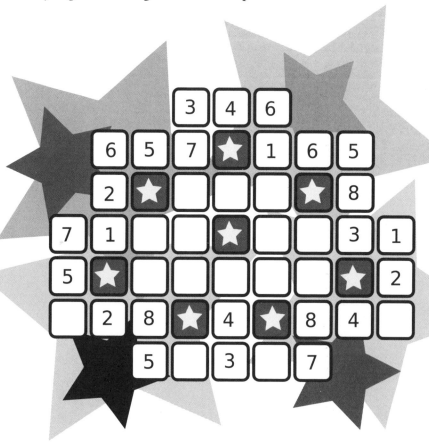

Trivia on the Brain

Most people can remember between 5 and 9 digits so long as they keep repeating the numbers to themselves. This is the limit of your working memory, the part of your memory you use to remember things in the short term.

Answers on page 187.

FIRING ON ALL CYLINDERS

Rhyme Time

GENERAL KNOWLEDGE   LANGUAGE

Answer each clue below with a pair of rhyming words. The numbers that follow each clue indicate how many letters are in each word. For example, "Plant seeds well underground (3, 3)" would be "sow low."

1. Plant seeds well underground (3, 3): _____

2. It occurred during dusting (3, 4): _____

3. How to get hot dirt (4, 4): _____

4. Information about a river (4, 4): _____

5. Tall Thai's garb (4, 6): _____

6. Where the plane crossed the Channel (4, 5): _____

7. Entrance to a waterway (6, 4): _____

8. Valid basis (5, 6): _____

9. Delay deciding for whom to vote (5, 6): _____

10. Fair-haired palm leaf (6, 5): _____

11. An invitation to play rugby (4, 5): _____

12. Last-ditch medicine? (7, 4): _____

13. As-yet-unsewn thread at the hospital (6, 6): _____

14. Gym-bag switch (6, 7): _____

15. Perk of a really clear night (7, 6): _____

16. More unusual park official (8, 6): _____

17. Problem with the paint job (7, 7): _____

18. Sydney zoo cleansing agent (8, 7): _____

Answers on page 187.

Sudoku

LOGIC

Use deductive logic to complete the grid so that each row, each column, and each 3×3 box contains the numbers 1 through 9 in some order. The solution is unique.

7	2	3	1	7	6	5	8	9
9	6	5	2	8	3	4	7	1
1	8	4	9	5	7	3	6	2
5	3	2	5	1	9	8	4	7
4	7	1	5	3	8	2	9	6
6	9	8	7	2	4	1	5	3
2	5	7	4	9	1	6	3	8
3	1	6	8	7	5	9	2	4
8	4	9	3	6	2	7	1	5

Multiples of Six
Number Maze

COMPUTATION   PLANNING

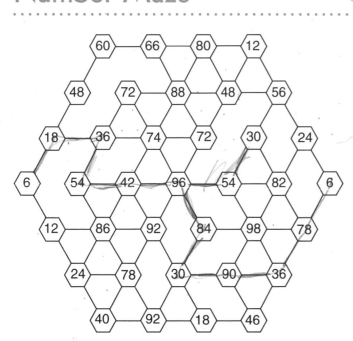

Find your way through the maze. Start with the hexagon containing a 6 on the left, and finish with the hexagon containing a 6 on the right. Move from hexagon to hexagon only if there is a line connecting them, and only pass through hexagons containing multiples of 6.

Answers on page 187.

Mirror, Mirror

There's no trick here, only a challenge: Draw the mirror image of each of these familiar objects. You may find it harder than you think!

Firing on All Cylinders

A Cross Earth

Every word in capital letters below is contained in the group of letters on page 141. They can be found in a straight line horizontally, vertically, or diagonally and may read either backward or forward. The leftover letters spell a related name (2 words).

AGRA (India)

APIA (Samoa)

ASPEN (Colorado)

ATLANTA (Georgia)

BALI (Indonesia)

BATH (England)

BERLIN (Germany)

BERN (Switzerland)

BOGOTA (Colombia)

BOISE (Idaho)

BONN (Germany)

BOSTON (Massachusetts)

BREST (France)

BUTTE (Montana)

CALI (Colombia)

CHAD (Africa)

CHICAGO (Illinois)

CORK (Ireland)

DALLAS (Texas)

GENOA (Italy)

GRAZ (Austria)

HOUSTON (Texas)

HOVE (England)

INDIANAPOLIS (Indiana)

JACKSON (Mississippi)

JENA (Germany)

JUNEAU (Alaska)

LAOS (Asia)

LAREDO (Texas)

LIEGE (Belgium)

LIMA (Peru)

LINCOLN (Nebraska)

LODI (New Jersey)

LOME (Togo)

MACON (Georgia)

MAN (Isle of)

MECCA (Saudi Arabia)

MESA (Arizona)

METZ (France)

MILAN (Italy)

MINNEAPOLIS (Minnesota)

MUMBAI (India)

NEW ORLEANS (Louisiana)

NEW YORK (New York)

NICE (France)

OHIO (U.S.A.)

OSLO (Norway)

PARA (Brazil)

PERTH (Australia)

PERU (South America)

PORTLAND (Oregon)   SAN FRANCISCO (California)
QUITO (Ecuador)   SANTA FE (New Mexico)
RABAT (Morocco)   SEATTLE (Washington)
RENO (Nevada)   SELMA (Alabama)
RIGA (Latvia)   SPOKANE (Washington)
ROME (Italy)   TALLAHASSEE (Florida)
ST. PETERSBURG (Florida)   TALLINN (Estonia)
SAN ANTONIO (Texas)

Leftover letters spell: _____

```
A N E J M                           O H I O S
R Z D U E Z S                   H I B U T T E
G A T N A L T A                 O N O O A P I A
A R B E A S P E N               U O I T S E R B M
  G D A L L A S M F             S T S A N T A F E
    I U T O T I U Q R       T N E M I E O O S
      R O D E R A L D A S O A L U C R N N A
        S I L O P A E N N I M E S E E
          U R E P N O A C B S B G R
            A E A S S A I U J
              W R S T I L R S A
            L O I T A S O G O N C C M
          O R D A H C P A G T R K O N A
        S M L S E L M A M E H O E S R S I N R
      M E E G E I L N I       A B O K R P L B O
    O G A C I H C A L         L N E W Y O R K M
  B B N T C A L I R           L A N N C K E E E
  A S A T A O D A             A N N N S A B E
  T A L L I N N               T M I L A N A
  H O V E I                     L O D I E
```

Answers on page 188.

Anagram Inventor

Find an anagram for each of the words on the right that will answer a clue on the left. Write the correct anagram on the line next to each clue. Then take the first letter of each anagram and combine them to spell the name of a great inventor.

Clues

1. King's seat _____

2. Annoy _____

3. Retro songs _____

4. Stately home _____

5. Kind of brick _____

6. Classified _____

7. Strolled _____

8. Become smaller _____

9. Leave, as a building _____

10. Monet, e.g. _____

11. _____ Hemingway _____

12. Scottish city _____

13. Pay no attention to _____

14. Fearful _____

15. Spaceship paths _____

16. Country _____

Anagram Words

abode

anoint

bistro

blamed

caveat

denude

hornet

lashes

lenses

region

resent

roman

sacred

soiled

stored

strait

Inventor: _____

Answers on page 188.

Odd-Even Logidoku

Use deductive logic to complete the grid so that each row, column, corner-to-corner diagonal, irregular shape, and 3×3 box contains the numbers 1 through 9 in some order. You may only place even numbers in boxes with the letter E. The solution is unique.

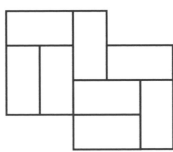

Word Jigsaw

Fit the pieces into the frame to form words reading across and down crossword-style. There is no need to rotate any of the pieces; they will fit as shown, with each piece used exactly once.

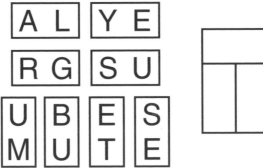

Answers on page 188.

Don's Diner and Part-Time Arcade

ATTENTION

We would never recommend that you eat at Don's Diner. Every time we've eaten there, something's gone completely crazy. Look at this picture of a typical lunch hour at Don's. We count 12 wrong things. How many can you find?

Number Translation

COMPUTATION   LOGIC

Each letter represents a different number from 1 through 9. Use the clues below to help you record the numbers in their correct places in the grid.

$G \times G = F + H$

$B \times G \times J = A$

$B \times D = D$

$D + D = G + J$

$E + H = B + C + F$

A	B	C
D	E	F
G	H	J

Answers on page 188.

Proverb Chains

Each chain below contains the letters that make up a familiar proverb. Begin with the indicated letter, and spell out each proverb by moving from letter to letter, but only if they are connected by a line. Use every letter in the chain at least once.

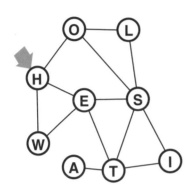

1. __ __   __ __ __ __

   __ __ __ __ __ __ __ __

   __ __   __ __ __ __.

2. __   __ __ __ __   __ __   __ __ __

   __ __ __ __   __ __   __ __ __ __

   __ __ __   __ __   __ __ __   __ __ __ __.

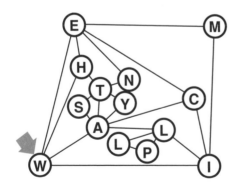

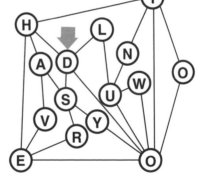

3. __ __ __ __   __ __ __   __ __ __'__

   __ __ __ __,   __ __ __

   __ __ __ __   __ __ __ __

   __ __ __ __.

4. __ __   __ __ __ __   __ __ __ __ __

   __ __   __ __ __   __ __ __ __

   __ __ __ __   __ __ __ __ __

   __ __   __ __ __ __   __ __ __.

Answers on page 188.

Let's Get Cooking!

ATTENTION

The cook has left a mess
of dots to be cleaned up.
How many do you count?

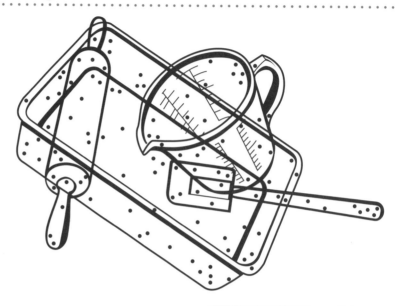

Animal Names

LANGUAGE   LOGIC

Cryptograms are messages in substitution code. For example, THE SMART CAT
might become FVO QWGDF JGF if **F** is substituted for **T, V** for **H, O** for **E,** and
so on. The code is the same for each animal name below. Break the code to reveal the
names.

1. T M D D Q D Q K C L N X

2. T C L X K V Y

3. U M Q J

4. F M Y C H H V

5. Y C I I M K

6. L Q N J K C M J F Q C K

7. V U V D T C J K

8. Q D Q X X N L

9. L Q Q X V

10. Y T M J Q O V Y Q X

Answers on page 188.

How Does Your Garden Grow?

Only 1 of these flowers appears an odd number of times. Can you find it?

Answer on page 188.

Sketchbook

Ambrose Anderson's granddaughter is at it again—sketching everything she sees. The top picture is a page from her sketchbook. But later on, she erased four of the drawings and replaced them with four new drawings. Study the top picture carefully, then turn the page upside-down to check out her revised sketchbook page. Without looking back at the top picture, can you circle the four drawings that are different?

Answers on page 189.

Equilateral Dismemberment

How many triangles are there in the larger figure? How many are there in the smaller figure? Are all of the triangles equilateral (all sides equal)?

Wise Wizard

LOGIC

An evil king has locked a wizard in a dungeon with nothing but a chair and a shovel. There is a window in the dungeon, but it's too high to reach using the chair. The dungeon is surrounded by a cement parking lot that stretches 100 feet in every direction. The wizard uses the shovel to dig a 50-foot-long tunnel and still manages to escape. How does he do it?

Answers on page 189.

Cubic Crazy

One of the figures cannot be folded to look like the centre object. Can you find it?

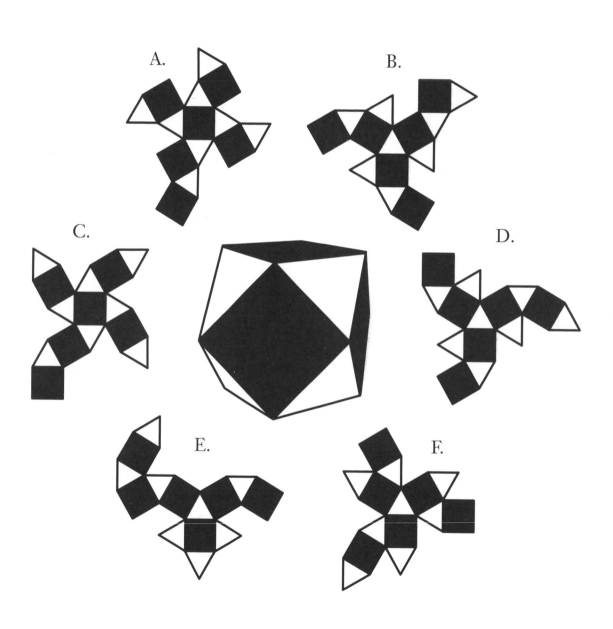

Answer on page 189.

150

Stack the Deck

This puzzle is actually 2 puzzles in 1. For the first puzzle, find a single, unbroken path from the outlined spade in the upper left corner to the outlined club in the lower right corner. You can only move diagonally, and you must alternate between spades and clubs as you move. For the second puzzle, start at the outlined heart in the upper right corner and alternate between hearts and diamonds to find an unbroken diagonal path to the outlined diamond in the lower left corner.

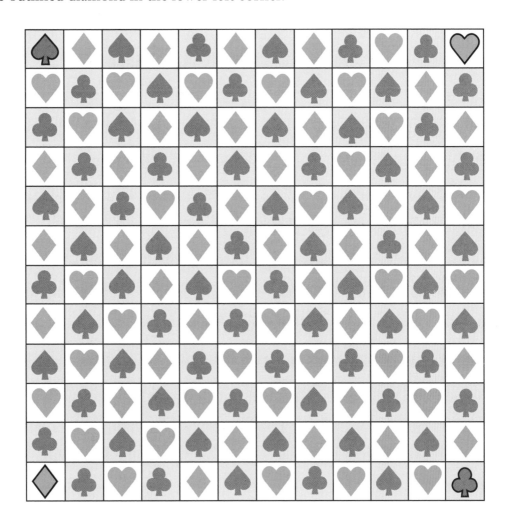

Answers on page 189.

A Startling Word Puzzle

LANGUAGE

What common English word can you think of that's 9 letters long and forms a new word every time you remove 1 letter from it? And what 8 other common English words can you form in this way? Think about it! The answer is startling.

Fruitcake?

alchemist?

STRINGIER?

⚙ Can You Repeat that Number One More Time?

Your memory can be divided into 3 categories: long-term memory, sensory memory, and short-term memory. Short-term memory refers to memories that last for just a few minutes. Your short-term memory has a limited capacity; it can only hold about 5 to 7 items (digits, words, letters) at one time. Once short-term memory items exceed this limit, new items you try to remember will begin to "shove out" older memories. So keep a pen handy, because your short-term memory can only remember that phone number for so long!

Shakespeare's Women

Every word listed is contained within the box of letters below. The words can be found in a straight line horizontally, vertically, or diagonally. They may read either backward or forward. The leftover letters spell the name of another one of Shakespeare's female characters (18 letters).

ALICE

ANDROMACHE

ANNE PAGE

AUDREY

BEATRICE

CASSANDRA

CELIA

CERES

CLEOPATRA

CORDELIA

CRESSIDA

DESDEMONA

DIANA

DOLL TEARSHEET

ELEANOR

ELIZABETH

EMILIA

GONERIL

```
L A R T A P O E L C L S R M L
J U L I E T G A C E D O I A E
U T C E T A C E H E N Y D R L
N N E E P E R C Y A R Y R I I
O P H E L I A O E N M E O N Z
R S N N H M T L L A C H S A A
C N A E O S E E C I R T A E B
A U D R E Y R B L R R N L U E
S D D I I A E A A A O E I I T
S N I S A T I I E M M E N M H
A N S S H N L L E T B M E O E
N A A A S U A D E R L I L G G
D O B G J E S S I C A L A E N
R J E D E E R H E R M I O N E
A I L E D R O C M I R A N D A
```

HECATE	JESSICA	LUCE	PERCY (Lady)
HERMIONE	JOAN	MARIANA	REGAN
IMOGEN	JULIA	MARINA	ROSALINE
IRAS	JULIET	MIRANDA	
IRIS	JUNO	NERISSA	Leftover letters:
ISABEL	LADY MACBETH	OPHELIA	

_____

Answers on page 189.

153

Firing on All Cylinders

A Tangle of Triangles

COMPUTATION

ANALYSIS   LOGIC

From studying the triangles below, can you find the missing number in the bottom triangle?

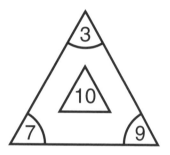 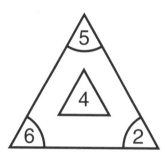 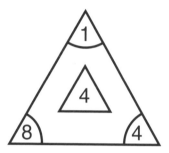

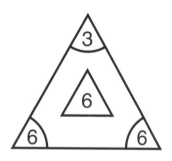 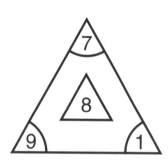 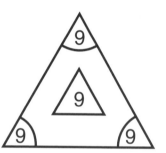

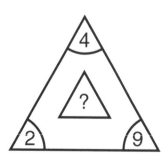

Answer on page 189.

Tourist Attraction

For each of the capitalized words, find an anagram that will answer one of the clues below. Write the correct anagram on the line by each clue. Then take the first letter of each anagram and combine them to spell the name of a tourist attraction.

ROVED	TRANCE	DOWRY	HENRI
TILES	ENEMY	TOILER	LACED
BELOW	REIGNS	VOILE	

Clues

1. English seaport   _____
2. Spot of land at sea   _____
3. Sinatra, e.g.   _____
4. Bee's drink   _____
5. Macaroni shape   _____
6. Arab country   _____
7. Talkative   _____
8. Shade of green   _____
9. European river   _____
10. Hang around   _____
11. Decorative sticker   _____

Tourist attraction: _____

Answers on page 189.

Mirror, Mirror

There's no trick here, only a challenge: Draw the mirror image of each of these familiar objects. You may find it harder than you think!

Word Jigsaw

Fit the pieces into the frame to form words reading across and down crossword-style. There is no need to rotate any of the pieces; they will fit as shown, with each piece used exactly once.

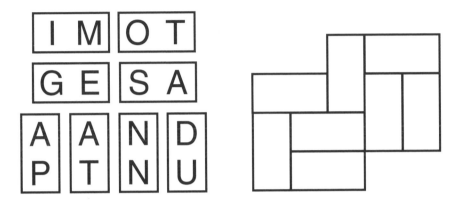

Headline Howlers

Cryptograms are messages in substitution code. For example, THE SMART CAT might become FVO QWGDF JGF if **F** is substituted for **T, V** for **H, O** for **E,** and so on. The code is the same for each cryptogram below. Break the code to read the headlines.

1. CGYW QVCB FZJIGJGEZW WFVMCW.

2. IBY JVDB OEXYW ZD FBK SIGYHBW.

3. VWJIEFVZJ JVCBW SXVQB PEI HVW GF WDVMBMIVPJ.

4. DXVFB JEE MXEWB JE HIEZFY, MIVWO DIESB JEXY.

Answers on page 189.

Rhyme Time

Answer each clue below with a pair or trio of rhyming words. The numbers that follow each clue indicate how many letters are in each word. For example, "What Adam gave to conceive Eve (3, 4)" would be "own bone."

1. What Adam gave to conceive Eve (3, 4): _____

2. Lover of custard dessert (4, 3): _____

3. Created riverbank deposits (5, 4): _____

4. Unexpected dam problem (5, 4): _____

5. Steal conduit (5, 4): _____

6. The hardest colour to see (5, 5): _____

7. Cynical escort (5, 5): _____

8. Desolate stream (5, 5): _____

9. Innumerable riches (6, 4): _____

10. Sufficiently brusque (5, 6): _____

11. Container for boiling water on a stove (5, 6): _____

12. Coating for a cozy country home (6, 5): _____

13. Captain Kirk's desire (7, 4): _____

14. Acrophobia (6, 6): _____

15. A desire to bungee jump one day (7, 5): _____

16. Investigator who looks inward (13, 9): _____

17. Totally fat-free milk source (9, 5): _____

18. Big bowl of pasta (6, 2, 7): _____

19. Stealth army getaway (8, 7): _____

20. Information you get from school (7, 9): _____

Answers on page 190.

Chip off the Old Block

Is A, B, C, D, or E the missing piece from the broken cube?

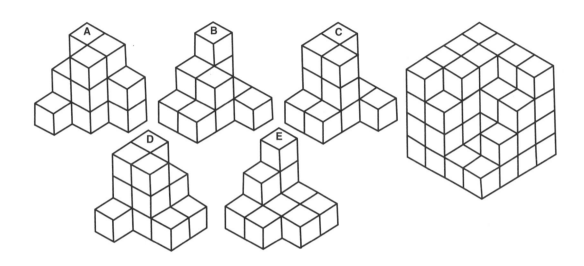

Petalgrams

LANGUAGE

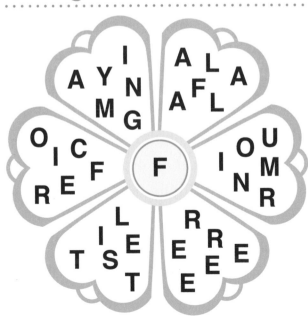

Form six 7-letter words using the letters in each petal plus the **F** in the centre. None of the words begins with **F**. Then, form a 7-letter bonus word (beginning with **F**) using the first letter of each word you made plus the **F**.

Answers on page 190.

Similar Lines

Each of these groups contains the letters of a simile. Decipher the similes by moving from letter to letter, but only if they are connected by a line. Some letters will be used more than once, and you may have to double back. Example: The simile "sly as a fox" is contained in the figure at right.

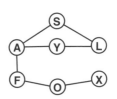

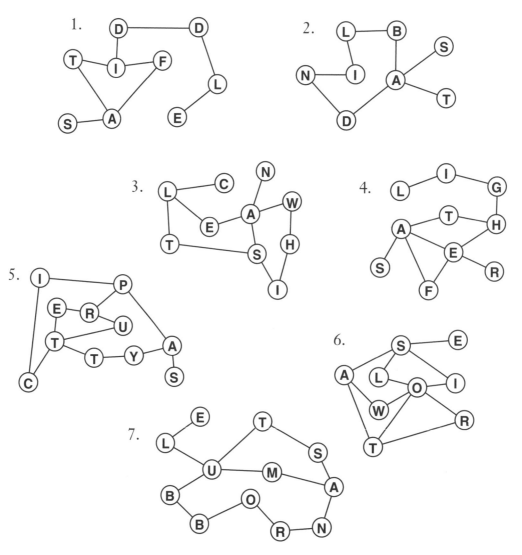

Answers on page 190.

Diamond in the Rough

Moving diagonally, can you find a single, unbroken path from the circle in the upper left corner to the circle in the lower right corner? Your path must move from circle to circle, with one twist: You can jump (in a straight line) over a diamond as long as there is a circle on the other side of it. There's only one way to complete the maze.

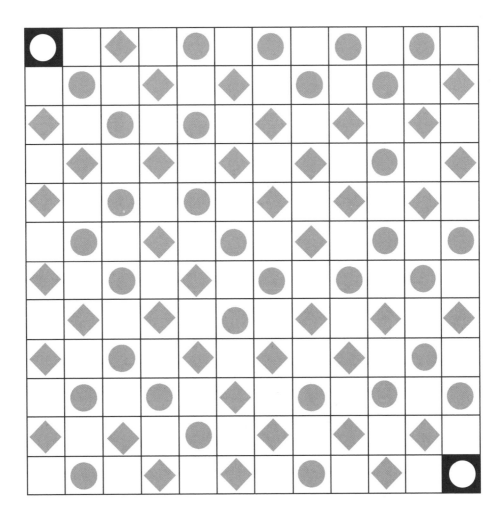

Answer on page 190.

Eat Your Words

ATTENTION **LANGUAGE** **VISUAL SEARCH**

Every phrase listed is contained within the group of letters on the next page. The phrases can be found horizontally, vertically, or diagonally. They may read either backward or forward.

A FINE KETTLE OF FISH

AN APPLE A DAY KEEPS
   THE DOCTOR AWAY

BRING HOME THE BACON

CAULIFLOWER EAR

COMPARE APPLES AND ORANGES

COOL AS A CUCUMBER

COUCH POTATO

CRY OVER SPILT MILK

FLAT AS A PANCAKE

HAPPY AS A CLAM

I HEARD IT THROUGH THE
   GRAPEVINE

IN A PICKLE

KNOW YOUR ONIONS

LIKE TWO PEAS IN A POD

NOT MY CUP OF TEA

PIE IN THE SKY

RED AS A BEET

SALT OF THE EARTH

SPILL THE BEANS

THAT'S THE WAY THE COOKIE
   CRUMBLES

THE PROOF IS IN THE PUDDING

THE WORLD IS YOUR OYSTER

TOP BANANA

WAKE UP AND SMELL THE
   COFFEE

WORK FOR PEANUTS

```
  L F L W C A E N         A       S
N O T H E O R E N V E I   C A U L I F
  O N P R I R O U I A N C O U R A A E
  C O L N C K M L V A T E W O I U A
  E A E A H A F F M E N T S A A B R S I T
  A O B P R N E O T N P I H K K N D T O A C H H A P E T K
    A E G E C E L R R T O A E C E E F O P F T A K T E R D U K H P T O P D E
    P T R H E T E A P C E R L F S U P A R R I U E A E L N C A U O W O K T R A A I O
    I C F A T A S Y S E C D G P N T P A O K A S L U S O E F H T A P L H A Y P F P K
    Y A O O R E A Y T P A A M E H K E A A H E F K I W N S R H Y A A A I A R O T L
    C U I F P O M W O E F N K N H E T O N A S P I Y F E I E T N A T E W E E L I T
      L N W T U P O W R Y R U B H T U E U D S O O N G L P U I A S H A T S A M T A
      I A A A T C O H F U O L T A B H Y S N S U R N E R O S R T E R T N E T H O T
      T T K L M S Y I G G O F F S L R G K L R M A S O K A W H Y O M A S L S T L A
      E E B C P S M L N O Y G L R I A U O U R E O A E E E E T O E A I T A R O
      A E R A I P O T T I R S S C S O N O O P F L P L W T C R B A P C T T R R
      T E B I F T O L O N R N I M H I R D R I F O L A C O T E E S B O P L H P
      R C N A G P A A T N E B M D O A N G S H W A Y T D E H L R A P O P O I W
      O G F S S I L M N H B A N L A K I O T T T T E H T O E E H R C A E A O
      O H B S A R C T F E U S V S R N P E C H T H W L E V S C O A A I N R R
      E O R A C D A E A A M T E L T O K K E R T I L R O C U A O F N W N D K
      Y M I L R L E T E A T L L H C I W C T S H I D Y O O O S E T F N U I F
      M N T O C V R I A P E E I L T O E P E P E R R C H C F H S C I C T O
      R G M D A F E K P S P T M E O E E H S E C U S A I T E F Y L C S S A
      K W F A A K C A L U I N B K H E A G T K A L U T E S O E E P O B H
        O S P M N E W D E N N I N K L N A H A A A S E K H R P P E B E
        E I F T R S D K N O E R Y U I A I E I N F H Y H P I M I H E
        E L E A B I T H A C V A N       N
        O A P N N C K   R I D           A
        L M C G P     U   A             B
      Y A O O     C B M P E A P     E L     P
        A A C         T A B N L K R I T H P W O Y B
    R E F           T K P L W P N N C R Y O V N T L C T T
    A B             O A E N P K E N B L T P P A Y E S A R O N O W
    E R             S T A O E I W E K A C N A P A S A T A L F A E L T O F O E
    L I             P N U G R N Y S A L T O F M O S P B T E E I S A H A P P B R I L
      I V C O O L A S A C U C U M B E R K N O W M A L C A S A Y P P A H O N S E S
    C F K N O       F L A E E U A I E E N S Y P U S I A P W A K E U P A N C L O
  E T H A R             T   P I E H A P P P A B U W A K E U P K N P
T E P I O                                       A A C P I
O L I K E                                       Y D S I M C
E N N A A                                       N A F P N E O
  W O R                                         R A A I H T
                                                O N O N A
                                                I E A A P
                                                A F I
```

Answers on page 190.

Take a Number!

COMPUTATION   LOGIC

Fill in the missing spaces with numbers from 1 through 9. The numbers in each row must add up to the number in the right-hand column. The numbers in each column must add up to the number on the bottom line. The numbers in the corner-to-corner diagonals must add up to the numbers in the upper and lower right corners.

43

2	3			5		2	9	1		47
3		8	7			2		3	8	41
	6	5	4		7	4			9	51
2		5	7	8		6	4		1	45
	2	9			6		8	9	1	51
7	4	3		2			5	5		35
	9	8	1	1		2	8			55
6	2		7		5	2		2	8	43
9				8	4	1	3	1	3	47
2		3	9	8	7			4	4	52
44	40	54	51	52	46	36	56	34	54	32

Answers on page 190.

Forget-Me-Not and Friends, Part I

We hereby nominate forget-me-not as the official flower of memory puzzles. Fill in the grid with the flower words. Then study the completed grid for 2 minutes to memorize the 12 words before turning the page for a quiz.

4 Letters

ALOE

5 Letters

DAISY

6 Letters

CACTUS

7 Letters

BOUQUET

JASMINE

8 Letters

DAFFODIL

HYACINTH

MAGNOLIA

MARIGOLD

9 Letters

BUTTERCUP

CARNATION

11 Letters

FORGET-ME-NOT

Answers on page 190.

165

Forget-Me-Not and Friends, Part II

MEMORY

(Don't read this until you've read the previous page!)

Circle the flower words that appeared in the grid on the previous page.

NOSEGAY

MAGNOLIA

LILAC

BUTTERCUP

JASMINE

LAVENDER

GLADIOLUS

DAFFODIL

CORNFLOWER

DAISY

FORGET-ME-NOT

JONQUIL

PERIWINKLE

CARNATION

PANSY

ALOE

Trivia on the Brain
The part of the brain called the amygdala gets its name from the Greek word for "almond" because of the similarities in shape.

Answers on page 190.

Stargazer

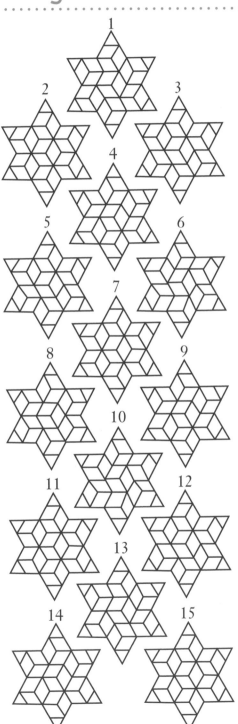

Look closely at these 15 stars. They may appear identical at first, but you'll find they're really not. Divide the stars into six groups of identical stars: Group I will contain four stars; Groups II and III will each contain three stars; Groups IV and V will each contain two stars; and Group VI will contain the only unique star.

Answers on page 190.

REASSESS YOUR BRAIN

You have just completed a set of puzzles designed to challenge your various mental skills. We hope you enjoyed them. Did this mental exercise also improve your memory, attention, problem solving, and other important cognitive skills? To get a sense of your improvement, please fill out this questionnaire. It is exactly the same as the one you filled out before you worked the puzzles in this book. So now you can compare your cognitive skills before and after you embarked on a *Brain Games*™ workout.

The questions below are designed to test your skills in the areas of memory, problem solving, creative thinking, attention, language, and more. Please reflect on each question, and rate your abilities on a 5-point scale, where 5 equals "excellent" and 1 equals "very poor." Then tally up your scores, and check out the categories at the bottom of the next page to learn how you have sharpened your brain.

1. You go to a large shopping centre with a list of different errands to run. Once inside, you realize you've forgotten to bring your list. How likely are you to get everything you need?

1   2   3   4   5

2. You've made an appointment with a doctor in an unfamiliar part of town. You printed out a map and directions, but once on the road you find that one of the streets you need to take is closed for construction. How well can you use your directions to find an alternate route?

1   2   3   4   5

3. You're nearly finished with a project when your boss changes the focus of the assignment but not the due date. How well can you juggle the work to accommodate the change?

1   2   3   4   5

4. How well can you remember everything you had for lunch the last three days?

1   2   3   4   5

5. You're driving to a new place. You need to concentrate on the directions, but the radio is on and your passenger wants to have a conversation. Can you devote the necessary attention to get to your location and chat with your passenger, while not missing the traffic report on the radio?

1   2   3   4   5

6. You're working on an assignment with a tight deadline, but your brother keeps calling to ask questions about the holiday you're taking together. Rate your ability to stay on task without getting distracted.

1   2   3   4   5

7. How good are you at remembering important dates, such as birthdays or anniversaries? (If you forget your anniversary, you're not just in the doghouse—you'll have to deduct points.)

1   2   3   4   5

8. When taking a family holiday, how good are you at fitting your family's luggage and supplies into the boot? Can you plan in advance the layout of the suitcases, or do you find yourself packing and unpacking several times on your departure date?

1   2   3   4   5

9. You have a long list for the supermarket but only have £30. How good are you at adding up the cost of essential items in your head so you don't go over once you get to the checkout?

1   2   3   4   5

10. You're hosting a reception, and you need to create a seating chart. You have to consider such factors as the available seating at each table, the importance of the guest, and the interpersonal relationships among the guests. How good are you at using logic to work out these complex seating arrangements?

1   2   3   4   5

10–25 Points:
Are You Ready to Make a Change?
Keep at it: There are plenty of activities that will help you improve your brain health! Continue working puzzles on a regular basis. Choose a different type of puzzle each day, or do a variety of them daily to help strengthen memory, focus attention, and improve logic and problem solving.

26–40 Points:
Building Your Mental Muscle
You're no mental slouch, but there's room to sharpen your mind! Try to identify the types of puzzles that you found particularly difficult in this book. Then you'll get an idea of which cognitive skills you need to work on. Remember, doing a puzzle can be the mental equivalent of doing sit-ups or squats: While they might not be your first choice of activity, you'll definitely like the results!

41–50 Points:
View from the Top
Congratulations! You have finished the puzzles in this book and are performing like a champion. To maintain this level of mental fitness, keep challenging yourself by working puzzles every day. Like the rest of the body's muscles, your mental strength can decline if you don't use it. So choose to keep your brain strong and active. You're at the summit—now you just have to stay to enjoy the view!

ANSWERS

Rhyme Time (page 11)
1. hot tot; 2. red sled; 3. ace place; 4. fake cake;
5. back rack; 6. bear chair; 7. news views;
8. funny money

Finding You (page 12)
YOUng Yoda found a yo-YO Under YOUr
Christmas tree. He tried to use it, but he looked
like a monkeY OUt of his tree. After hitting his
head, he called his YOUthful friend Yoric and
said, "HurrY, OUch!" Yoric rode the TokYO
Underground all the way to YOUngstown, whistling the dittY "O Ulysses." "YOU're in luck,
Yoda," said Yoric, "I'm a yo-YO User, too." Yoric
taught Yoda to yo-yo, and in appreciation Yoda
took some candY OUt and gave it to his friend.

Sudoku (page 12)

3	5	1	7	8	9	2	6	4
4	2	7	6	3	5	8	9	1
6	9	8	1	4	2	7	3	5
2	7	4	9	6	3	5	1	8
9	3	5	4	1	8	6	7	2
1	8	6	5	2	7	9	4	3
5	4	9	8	7	1	3	2	6
7	6	2	3	5	4	1	8	9
8	1	3	2	9	6	4	5	7

Gone Fishin' (page 13)
1. river running uphill; 2. fishing line behind
bridge; 3. perspective on floor tiles is wrong;
4. top and bottom of barrel showing; 5. man on
hill touching man in window; 6. impossibly large
bird on tree

Name Calling (page 13)
WEALTH

Count on This! (page 14)

				15
1	9	7	6	23
8	7	3	5	23
6	4	8	9	27
2	2	1	5	10
17	22	19	25	21

Word Ladder (page 14)
Answers may vary.
BALL, gall, gale, GAME

Thirsty? (page 15)

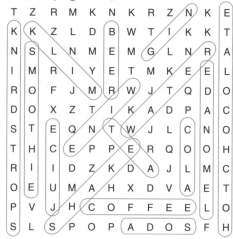

Quilt Quest (page 16)

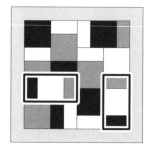

170

Answers

Hello, My Name Is Wrong (page 16)
Morey Munny and Les Thyme

Word Jigsaw (page 17)

Geometric Shapes (page 17)

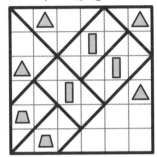

Where Are the Animals? (page 18)
1. dog/cat; 2. skunk/elk; 3. deer/owl; 4. fox/snake; 5. wolf/horse; 6. rabbit/elephant; 7. tiger/lion; 8. monkey/eagle; 9. seal/whale; 10. parrot/eel

Flying High (page 19)

COANFL	FALCON
RIOBN	ROBIN
CAALINRD	CARDINAL
NAARYC	CANARY
BIRDULEB	BLUEBIRD
WOCR	CROW
EGLAE	EAGLE
WSROPRA	SPARROW
GASLIRNT	STARLING

FREE AS A BIRD

Time Capsule (page 20)
"I went to a restaurant that serves 'breakfast at any time,' so I ordered French toast during the Renaissance."
—Steven Wright

Jumbled Idiom (page 20)
FAUCET CHIMES = FACE THE MUSIC

Word Columns (page 21)

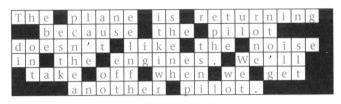

The plane is returning because the pilot doesn't like the noise in the engines. We'll take off when we get another pilot.

Name Calling (page 21)
GRAVITY

Seven Slices (page 22)

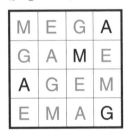

Game On! (page 22)

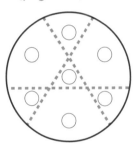

Rhyme Time (page 23)
1. ray bay; 2. far star; 3. same name; 4. Rome home; 5. half laugh; 6. wide slide

Word Jigsaw (page 23)

Answers

Fish Fantasy (page 25)

Backyard Barbecue (page 26)

WET SIGNS = SWING SET
HOSE SHORES = HORSESHOES
TOAST PIE = PATIO SET
EAGLE CUSHION = CHAISE LONGUE
SHORE COOP = HOROSCOPE
GAIN MAZE = MAGAZINE
RUM LABEL = UMBRELLA
NO HBO CONCERT = CORN ON THE
    COB
PRESCRIBE MAD HUB = BARBECUED
    SHRIMP
TO CHOKE SKIS = KISS THE COOK

The Good Book (page 26)

The missing letter is "M." The sequence is
Matthew, Mark, Luke, John.

The Fruit Vendor's Cart (page 27)

Max and Mitch (page 28)

1. C. ELECTRIC GUITAR
2. D. SAXOPHONE
3. F. DRUM MAJORETTE
4. B. TAMBOURINE
5. E. HARMONICA
6. A. ACCORDION

Geometric Shapes (page 28)

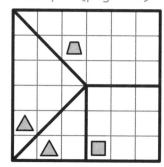

Layer by Layer (page 29)

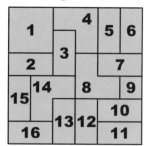

Word Ladder (page 29)

Answers may vary.
REAL, seal, seam, SHAM

Fitting Words (page 30)

P	A	R	I	S
E	R	O	D	E
A	C	T	O	R
S	H	E	L	F

Name Calling (page 30)

SKATE

Layer by Layer (page 31)

First Song (page 31)

1. Star-Spangled Banner
2. national anthem

At the Movies (pages 32–33)

Shall We Dance? (page 34)

1. F. FOLK DANCE
2. D. BELLY DANCE
3. B. BREAK DANCE
4. E. SQUARE DANCE
5. A. FLAMENCO
6. C. TAP DANCE

Star Power (page 35)

Word Ladder (page 35)

STARS, stare, share, shire, SHINE

A Bit Askew (page 36)

The But-Not Game (page 36)

Carol likes words with alternating consonants and vowels.

See Your Name in Print! (page 38)

YOUR NAME

It's Old (page 38)

The first letter is **G,** as in Genesis. The sequence is Genesis, Exodus, Leviticus, Numbers, Deuteronomy (the first five books of the Old Testament).

Answers

Rhyme Time (page 39)

1. ode code; 2. old cold; 3. hot yacht; 4. ocean motion; 5. dark park; 6. nail sale; 7. sword cord; 8. small haul; 9. black lack; 10. great bait *or* sure lure; 11. beam team; 12. chief thief; 13. terse verse; 14. fair éclair; 15. school pool

Crazy Mixed-Up Letters (page 40)

hornets, shorten, thrones

Let's Make Some Music (page 41)

1	2	3	4	5	6	7	8	9	10	11	12	13
G	H	P	I	A	N	O	J	W	T	X	K	F
14	15	16	17	18	19	20	21	22	23	24	25	26
D	R	U	M	Z	L	S	B	E	C	V	Y	Q

X-Hibit of X's (page 42)

1. X-ray; 2. xylophone; 3. xylophonist

Sudoku (page 42)

9	3	2	5	7	1	4	6	8
4	5	7	8	6	2	1	9	3
1	8	6	9	3	4	2	5	7
7	4	9	3	2	6	8	1	5
2	1	5	7	9	8	6	3	4
3	6	8	1	4	5	9	7	2
6	9	4	2	5	3	7	8	1
8	7	3	4	1	9	5	2	6
5	2	1	6	8	7	3	4	9

Inching Along (page 43)

IN CHina, INCHworms are used in a pINCH when fishing for perch IN CHannels. ZINC Has also been used, especially if the perch IN CHannels are susceptible to colds. One fisherman using INCHworms caught so many perch, he had to clINCH his boat to his truck with a wINCH and INCH it up the bank. A goldfINCH flew in his window and made him flINCH, but he did nothing because IN CHina it's against the law to lynch a fINCH.

Sum Fun (page 43)

						30
9	3	5	4	7	3	**31**
2	1	2	8	2	8	**23**
1	6	4	1	9	3	**24**
7	3	7	2	1	6	**26**
4	9	8	6	4	5	**36**
8	5	9	5	7	1	**35**
31	**27**	**35**	**26**	**30**	**26**	**21**

Between the Lines (page 44)

1. a) food, b) fool, c) foot
2. a) grove, b) grow, c) growl
3. a) withhold, b) without, c) withstand
4. a) watch, b) water, c) watt

"Fools grow without watering."
—Thomas Fuller

Ubiquity of U's (page 45)

1. umbrella; 2. underwear; 3. unicorn; 4. unicycle; 5. unicyclist; 6. Union Jack; 7. upholstery (on the chairs); 8. utensils

How Will You Conduct Yourself? (page 46)

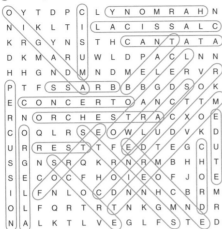

Word Ladder (page 47)

Answers may vary.
BEAR, dear, deal, dell, dull, BULL

Count Down (page 47)

					32
1	5	5	8	4	**23**
1	3	2	9	5	**20**
7	2	2	4	8	**23**
3	8	7	7	1	**26**
9	9	3	3	2	**26**
21	**27**	**19**	**31**	**20**	**15**

Tessellated Floor (page 48)

Word Jigsaw (page 48)

```
      A T E
  O A K E N
    D R I E D
    D E N
```

Number Challenge (page 49)

2	1	■	6	1
2	3	4	5	6
■	7	7	5	■
7	9	3	5	1
7	5	■	6	5

Triple-Jointed (pages 50–51)

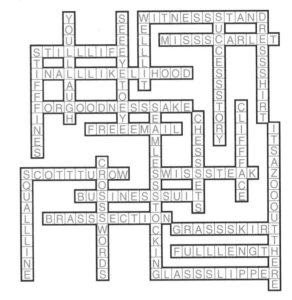

Extra-Credit Answer: All the words contain 3 identical letters in a row.

Letters to Numbers (page 52)

A **8**	B **1**	C **6**
D **3**	E **5**	F **7**
G **4**	H **9**	J **2**

Answers

Copycats (page 52)

Animal Farm (page 53)

NEED I ERR = REINDEER
SHOPPERS RAG = GRASSHOPPER
GLARING BEET = BENGAL TIGER
NEAT HELP = ELEPHANT
MESH TAR = HAMSTER
LEG RIB = GERBIL
GOLF DISH = GOLDFISH
EGO NIP = PIGEON
PALE NOTE = ANTELOPE

Match-Up Twins (page 54)

The matching pairs are 1 and 8, 2 and 9, 3 and 6, 4 and 7, and 5 and 10.

Rhyme Time (page 55)

1. mean queen; 2. play day; 3. same name; 4. bite tight; 5. lame claim; 6. very hairy; 7. fair share; 8. maybe baby; 9. wrong song; 10. chief grief; 11. court sport; 12. spare chair; 13. appear near; 14. jacket racket; 15. candle scandal

Word Columns (page 56)

In some societies, they beat the ground with clubs and yell. It is called witchcraft. Other societies call it "golf."

Back at You (page 56)

A mirror

Grab Bag (page 57)

1. D. SNOW GLOBE
2. A. TOY SOLDIER
3. E. AFRICA DESIGN
4. C. BONSAI
5. B. FISHBOWL

Fitting Words (page 58)

Word Ladder (page 58)

Answers may vary.
HAIR, hail, hall, ball, BALD

City Sites (page 59)

La Scala — Milan
Taj Mahal — Agra
Basin Street — New Orleans
Left Bank — Paris
Colosseum — Rome
Piccadilly Circus — London
Kremlin — Moscow
Forbidden City — Beijing
Ginza — Tokyo
Moro Castle — Havana

Tamagram (page 59)

ITALIC END = IDENTICAL

Quilt Quest (page 60)

Word Jigsaw (page 60)

Bears Repeating (page 61)

Wacky Wordy (page 61)

Once in a blue moon

Bungle Gym (page 62)

BROW CLOTH = BLOWTORCH
CRUCIAL WARS = CIRCULAR SAW
I WAS CHAN = CHAIN SAW
WEB ATLAS = TABLE SAW
LOGIC SPRINKLE = LOCKING PLIERS
CAR BROW = CROWBAR

Alternate Universe? (page 62)

In a dictionary

Born in 1875 (page 63)

He was born in Room 1875 in the hospital, not in the year 1875.

Sudoku (page 63)

Horsing Around (pages 64–65)

Theme: The first word in each phrase can be paired with "horse" to make a new expression.

Misleading Sequence (page 66)

12 + 6 = 18

Missing Connections (page 66)

Answers

Sloop John B. and Co. (pages 67–68)
frigate, dory, barge, yacht, canoe, outrigger, ferry, sloop, junk

Toys (page 68)
Child 1 received the 58P toy and a 95P toy for a total of £1.53. Child 2 received a 25P toy, a 41P toy, and an 87P toy for a total of £1.53. This left child 3 with the 27P and 30P toys.

Hidden Critters (page 69)
1. SHE EPitomizes elegance.
2. Soap is anTI-GERm.
3. He maDE ERrors.
4. Urban reneWAL RUShes on.
5. He did the taSK UNKnowingly.
6. Her BADGE Revealed her mission.
7. I went TO A Dandy party.
8. Smell neW OLFactory sensations.
9. Would you reBUFF A LOcal swain?
10. Yes, iF ROGer will.

Digital Sudoku (page 70)

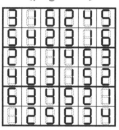

Fitting Words (page 70)

F	I	L	T	H
A	D	I	E	U
T	O	M	E	S
S	L	O	S	H

Number Crossword (page 71)

		2	1
7	6	5	4
2	8	6	4
9	2		

Word Columns (page 71)

I got a great bargain the other day when I bought a forklift for half-price. It's amazing what you can pick up these days.

Rhyme Time (page 72)
1. blue gnu; 2. crop swap; 3. stray ray; 4. cheaper keeper; 5. snack rack; 6. sole goal; 7. full bull; 8. sable label; 9. later gator; 10. short report; 11. slower grower; 12. worn horn; 13. complete fleet; 14. history mystery

Swimming with the Cubes (page 73)
The answer is C.

Between the Lines (pages 74–75)
1. a) sharp, b) sharpen, c) sharp-eyed
2. a) lovable, b) love, c) lovely
3. a) preselect, b) presence, c) present
4. a) abscond, b) absence, c) absent
5. a) strength, b) strengthen, c) strenuous
"Absence sharpens love, presence strengthens it."
—Thomas Fuller

Motel Hideout (page 76)
The thief is in room 25.

Diagonal Switch (page 77)

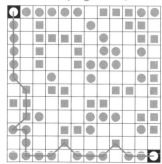

Fitting Words (page 78)

F	I	R	S	T
I	R	A	T	E
J	O	K	E	S
I	N	E	P	T

A Sign of the Times (page 78)

				40
3	3	2	4	72
4	5	2	1	40
3	5	4	3	180
1	1	5	5	25
36	75	80	60	300

What's for Dinner? (page 79)

In the bottom picture: 1. rounded chair back;
2. girl has soldier toy; 3. girl wearing black skirt;
4. bowl on plate in front of girl; 5. sailboat flag
pointing right; 6. man wearing bow tie; 7. man
holding screwdriver; 8. ham on platter; 9. corn
on table; 10. jug half full; 11. cake on windowsill;
12. window has two panes; 13. square pattern on
curtain; 14. boy wearing jumper; 15. potatoes in
bowl are not mashed; 16. woman not wearing
oven gloves; 17. woman wearing different apron;
18. tray cover is square

All the Colours of the Rainbow (pages 80–81)

All the Colours of the Rainbow, cont.

Leftover letters spell: RED, ORANGE, YEL-
LOW, GREEN, BLUE, INDIGO, VIOLET

Word Columns (page 82)

I	b	e	l	i	e	v	e		f	o	r		e	v	e	r	y		d	r	o	p
o	f		r	a	i	n		t	h	a	t		f	a	l	l	s	,		a		
		f	l	o	w	e	r		g	r	o	w	s	,		a						
f	o	u	n	d	a	t	i	o	n		l	e	a	k	s	,		a		b	a	l	l
g	a	m	e		g	e	t	s		r	a	i	n	e	d		o	u	t	,		a	
	c	a	r		r	u	s	t	s		a	n	d					.	.			

Find the Booty! (page 82)

1. E N T E R T A I N
2. T H O U S A N D S
3. S U P E R S T A R
ERT + USA + ERS = TREASURES

Overload of O's (page 83)

obelisk, octagon, octopus, oil can, olives, onion,
ostrich, ottoman, outboard engine, outlet, oven

All Together Now (page 83)

The next letter is "R." The sequence is J, P, G,
R, as in John, Paul, George, and Ringo—the
members of the Beatles.

Take 30 (page 84)

Alf turned the candle on its side and balanced
it on the candleholder. Then he lit the wick at
both ends. The flames met in the middle exactly
30 minutes later.

Scrambled Squares (page 84)

T	O	K	E	N
B	L	A	D	E
S	T	A	N	D
A	U	R	A	L
S	N	I	P	S

S	T	R	I	F	E
B	R	O	K	E	N
I	N	S	E	R	T
A	S	S	E	R	T
C	A	N	T	E	R
R	E	P	E	A	T

Answers

Car Chase (page 85)

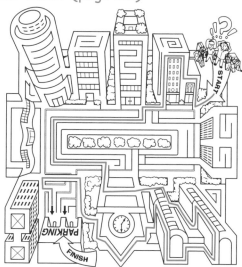

Times Squared (page 86)

6	3	2	1	36
1	3	7	7	147
5	1	5	5	125
8	3	1	3	72

240 27 70 105

Letter Quilt (page 86)

D	C			A	B
A		B	D	C	
C	D	A			B
B			C	D	A
	A	D	B		C
	B	C	A		D

Famous Address (page 87)

Four score and seven years ago

Word Ladders (page 87)

Answers may vary.
1. HAIR, hail, bail, ball, bale, bare, CARE
2. CUP, cap, tap, tan, ten, TEA

Unbearable Jigsaw (page 89)

Planks Galore (page 90)

There are 18 boards in each cube, for a total of 36 boards.

Logidoku (page 90)

7	4	6	1	5	2	8	3
1	6	4	3	7	8	2	5
5	3	8	2	6	1	4	7
8	2	7	5	4	3	1	6
2	5	3	8	1	6	7	4
3	1	5	7	2	4	6	8
4	7	2	6	8	5	3	1
6	8	1	4	3	7	5	2

ABCD (page 91)

			A	0	1	3	1	2	2
			B	2	1	1	2	2	1
			C	2	3	1	1	0	2
A	B	C	D	2	1	1	2	2	1
1	2	2	1	B	C	A	B	D	C
1	2	2	1	C	B	D	C	A	B
2	1	1	2	D	C	A	D	B	A
1	1	2	2	C	D	C	B	A	D
1	1	2	2	D	C	A	D	B	C
3	2	0	1	B	A	B	A	D	A

Let Freedom Ring (page 91)

Born on the Fourth of July

Cube Fold (page 92)

Figure 8

Cross Count (page 93)

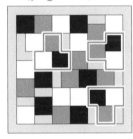

Cast-a-word (page 93)

Die 1: A, H, L, S, X, Z
Die 2: B, E, G, K, P, Q
Die 3: C, D, F, O, T, Y
Die 4: I, J, M, N, R, U

Quilt Quest (page 94)

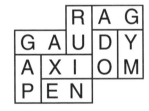

Word Jigsaw (page 94)

```
    R A G
G A U D Y
A X I O M
P E N
```

Fun with Numbers (page 95)

The number is 741.

Famous Last Line (page 95)

Louis, I think this is the beginning of a beautiful friendship.

Star Power (page 96)

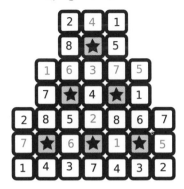

Vocal Vowels (page 96)

Argentinean

Word Jigsaw (page 97)

```
      F O E
S T O N E
P I X E L
A N Y
```

Face the Blocks (page 97)

A=1, B=1, C=2, D=2, E=1, F=1, G=3, H=2, I=3, J=2, K=5, L=3

Red, White, and Blue (page 98)

	A	B	C	D	E	F
1	R	W	R	B	B	W
2	B	W	B	R	W	R
3	W	R	W	R	B	B
4	R	B	R	B	W	W
5	W	B	B	W	R	R
6	B	R	W	W	R	B

Answers

Cast-a-word (page 99)
Die 1: A, D, I, K, N, V
Die 2: B, E, M, P, S, T
Die 3: C, F, J, Q, R, Y
Die 4: G, H, L, O, U, W

Word Columns (page 99)

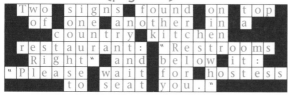

Last Laugh Department (pages 100–101)

1. Agatha Christie's first book, *The Mysterious Affair at Styles*, which introduced her Belgian detective Hercule Poirot, was rejected by the first six publishers she submitted it to.
2. John Grisham's first novel, *A Time to Kill*, was rejected by twenty-eight publishers.
3. Robert W. Pirsig's *Zen and the Art of Motorcycle Maintenance* was rejected—ouch!—one hundred and twenty-one times before it became a bestseller for Morrow in nineteen seventy-four.
4. Ayn Rand's *The Fountainhead* was rejected by the first twelve publishers she approached.
5. J. K. Rowling's first book, *Harry Potter and the Philosopher's Stone*, was turned down by nine publishers, including HarperCollins and Penguin, before Bloomsbury signed it up.
6. Dr. Seuss's first children's book, *And to Think That I Saw It on Mulberry Street*, was rejected by twenty-six publishers before it was published in nineteen thirty-seven.

Merit Badge (page 102)

Biff will need 3 other Scouts to go with him. Each will carry a 5-day supply of food and water. After the first day of hiking, the first Scout accompanying Biff will give 1 day of supplies each to Biff and the other 2 Scouts, using his last 1-day supply to hike back home. Each remaining Scout will then have a 5-day supply. After the second day, the second Scout will give Biff and the third Scout 1 day of supplies each and use his remaining 2-day supply to hike back home. Biff and the third Scout will once again each have 5 days of supplies. After the third day of hiking, the third Scout will give Biff 1 day of supplies and use his remaining 3 days of supplies to hike back home. Biff will be left with 5 days of supplies, enough to complete his 8-day hike and get the merit badge.

Logidoku (page 102)

6	8	9	3	5	1	4	2	7
2	1	4	8	7	9	6	3	5
5	3	7	2	4	6	1	9	8
3	4	6	5	1	8	9	7	2
1	5	2	7	9	3	8	4	6
7	9	8	6	2	4	3	5	1
8	6	5	4	3	7	2	1	9
9	2	3	1	6	5	7	8	4
4	7	1	9	8	2	5	6	3

Roman Numerals Challenge (page 103)

$\overline{\text{XCMX}}$ CMLXXXIX

Fitting Words (page 103)

Answers

My Kind of Town (pages 104–105)

Theme: The terms are either songs performed in the movie *Chicago* or songs recorded by the rock band Chicago.

Rhyme Time (page 106)

1. found pound; 2. third herd; 3. attack back;
4. cheer dear; 5. whist twist; 6. string ring;
7. older folder; 8. turkey jerky; 9. elder welder;
10. groovy movie; 11. dinner winner; 12. wander yonder; 13. tougher buffer; 14. winter sprinter;
15. truffle scuffle; 16. lighter fighter; 17. rounder flounder; 18. complete retreat

Logidoku (page 107)

5	9	2	3	4	1	6	8	7
4	7	8	6	2	5	3	1	9
6	3	1	7	8	9	4	2	5
8	1	3	4	7	2	9	5	6
2	5	7	9	6	8	1	4	3
9	6	4	5	1	3	8	7	2
7	4	9	8	5	6	2	3	1
1	8	6	2	3	7	5	9	4
3	2	5	1	9	4	7	6	8

Word Jigsaw (page 107)

Counting Up (page 108)

The next number is 50. These numbers represent the value of British pence.

Geometric Shapes (page 108)

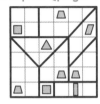

Number-Crossed (page 109)

	4	9	5	
5	5	1	4	4
1	6		3	8
2	7	3	2	4
	8	4	1	

Flower Shop (page 110)

In the bottom picture: 1. no stripe on umbrella cap; 2. pom-poms on every other gather of umbrella; 3. tulips are all dark; 4. only 1 sunflower; 5. different flowers in spotted vase; 6. mums in striped basket; 7. stripes on rose pail horizontal; 8. wheels different on cart; 9. no flowers on bottom of cart; 10. handle on cart pail in other direction; 11. no stripes on cart bucket; 12. woman has open mouth; 13. woman has short sleeves; 14. woman wearing bracelets; 15. woman handing girl different type of flower; 16. girl's hair different; 17. girl's sleeves are capped; 18. girl wearing pants; 19. no "for" in sign; 20. singular "flower" on sign; 21. cobblestones running in different direction

Jigstars (page 111)

The pairs are A and G, B and K, C and F, D and L, E and H, and I and J.

183

Answers

Four Sisters (page 112)

Robert is not married to Roberta (Clue 1), Paula (Clue 2), or Alberta (Clue 3), so his wife is Carla. Albert is not married to Alberta (Clue 1) or Roberta (Clue 3), so his wife is Paula. Paul is not married to Roberta (Clue 2), so his wife is Alberta. Therefore, Carl's wife must be Roberta, whose last name is not Carlson or Robertson (Clue 1) or Paulson (Clue 4); it is Albertson. Robert and Carla's last name is not Robertson or Carlson (Clue 1), so it is Paulson. Since Robert Paulson is not the man in the second half of Clue 3, Robertson is the last name of Albert and Paula. This leaves Carlson as the last name of Paul and Alberta.

In summary:

Alberta	Paul	Carlson
Carla	Robert	Paulson
Paula	Albert	Robertson
Roberta	Carl	Albertson

Crisscross Puzzle (page 113)

Fair Freddy's Fondue Fete (page 114)

He needs to cut 42 bread cubes ($2 \times 3 \times 7 = 42$).

Times Squared (page 114)

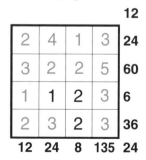

Word Ladders (page 115)

Answers may vary.
1. CORN, torn, tern, term, team, teas, PEAS
2. PRAYER, brayer, braver, beaver, heaver, HEAVEN

You Can't Have a Slice of This . . . (page 115)

The answer is "N," as in "Nine." The letter sequence stands for Three, One, Four, One, Five, Nine: 3.14159, the first 6 digits of pi.

Classic Lit (page 116)

"It is a truth universally acknowledged, that a single man in possession of a good fortune, must be in want of a wife."
—Jane Austen, *Pride and Prejudice*

Fitting Words (page 117)

M	A	C	A	W
A	L	I	B	I
L	O	T	U	S
T	E	E	T	H

Letter Quilt (page 118)

	D		B	A	C
A	C		D		B
D	B	A		C	
		B	C	D	A
C		D	A	B	
B	A	C			D

X × IV (page 118)

W-Cubed Rectangles (page 119)

Patterns C and D can be folded to form the cube.

Answers

Star Power (page 120)

Plus and Minuses (page 121)

123 − 45 − 67 + 89 = 100

Circles and Numbers (page 121)

The number 2 should be substituted for the question mark in the upper right circle, because the numbers encompassed by each of the circles in the illustration add up to 25.

A Four-midable Maze (page 122)

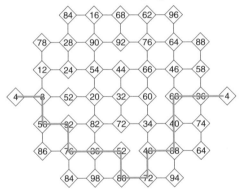

Three for Two (page 123)

Answers may vary.
1. **CAR**ROT, ES**CAR**GOT;
2. **ERI**E, SUP**ERI**OR;
3. SEPTE**MBE**R, NOVE**MBE**R;
4. SA**HARA**, KALA**HARI**;
5. HUN**GARY**, BUL**GARIA**

M Is for Mystery (page 125)

Man of Steel Chalet = The Maltese Falcon; Hag at Charities = Agatha Christie; Our Helicopter = Hercule Poirot; Simple Arms = Miss Marple; My Spiderwort Eel = Lord Peter Wimsey; Guinea Dustup = Auguste Dupin; Glad Aeroplane = Edgar Allan Poe; Chilean Arch = Charlie Chan. Give yourself bonus points if your keen deductive powers revealed Shellshock Rome as Sherlock Holmes, whose devoted friend, Two-Star Condo, was his chronicler, Doctor Watson.

Wacky Wordy (page 126)

Drawing on the right side of the brain

It's a Song (page 126)

One for the money, two for the show

Geometric Shapes (page 127)

Word Jigsaw (page 127)

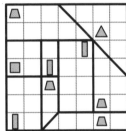

Star Power (page 128)

Answers

Around Five Cubes (page 129)

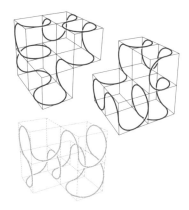

Diagonal Jump (page 130)

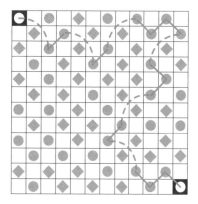

Geometric Shapes (page 131)

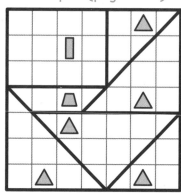

Shoe Sale (page 132)

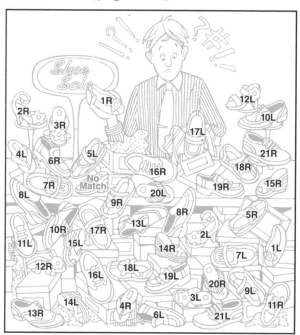

Cross Count (page 133)

R$_9$	O$_6$	B$_2$	E$_5$	22
E$_5$	V$_4$	I$_9$	L$_3$	21
S$_1$	E$_5$	T$_2$	S$_1$	9
T$_2$	R$_9$	E$_5$	E$_5$	21
17	24	18	14	

Coffee Break (page 133)

Note that 12 percent is the same as $\frac{3}{25}$. Fill the 5-cup cafetiere with water, and dissolve the coffee packet in it. This liquid has a coffee concentration of 20 percent, or $\frac{1}{5}$. Pour 3 cups from the 5-cup cafetiere into the 3-cup one. Discard the remaining 2 cups from the 5-cup cafetiere. Pour the liquid from the 3-cup cafetiere into the 5-cup one. The 3-cups-worth of liquid in the 5-cup cafetiere contains $\frac{3}{5}$ of a cup of actual coffee. Fill the remainder of the 5-cup cafetiere with water to dilute the liquid to a coffee concentration of $\frac{3}{5}$ of a cup out of 5 cups, or $\frac{3}{25}$, which is 12 percent.

Answers

Road Trip! (page 134)

Odd-Even Logidoku (page 135)

Quilt Quest (page 135)

Star Power (page 136)

Rhyme Time (page 137)

1. sow low; 2. rag snag; 3. boil soil; 4. Nile file;
5. long sarong; 6. over Dover; 7. strait gate;
8. sound ground; 9. await debate; 10. blonde
frond; 11. come scrum; 12. obscure cure;
13. future suture; 14. duffle shuffle; 15. amazing
gazing; 16. stranger ranger; 17. peeling ceiling;
18. kangaroo shampoo

Sudoku (page 138)

7	2	3	1	4	6	5	8	9
9	6	5	2	8	3	4	7	1
1	8	4	9	5	7	3	6	2
5	3	2	6	1	9	8	4	7
4	7	1	5	3	8	2	9	6
6	9	8	7	2	4	1	5	3
2	5	7	4	9	1	6	3	8
3	1	6	8	7	5	9	2	4
8	4	9	3	6	2	7	1	5

Multiples of Six Number Maze (page 138)

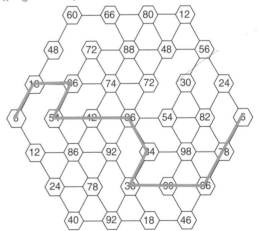

Answers

A Cross Earth (pages 140–141)

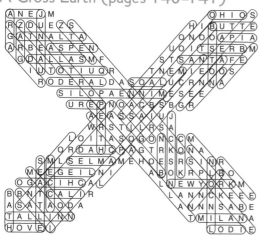

Leftover letters spell: Mediterranean Sea

Anagram Inventor (page 142)

1. throne/hornet; 2. hassle/lashes; 3. oldies/soiled; 4. manor/roman; 5. adobe/abode; 6. sorted/stored; 7. ambled/blamed; 8. lessen/lenses; 9. vacate/caveat; 10. artist/strait; 11. Ernest/resent; 12. Dundee/denude; 13. ignore/region; 14. scared/sacred; 15. orbits/bistro; 16. nation/anoint

Inventor: Thomas Alva Edison

Odd-Even Logidoku (page 143)

Word Jigsaw (page 143)

S	U	B	
U	S	U	A	L
M	E	R	G	E
	Y	E	T	

Don's Diner and Part-Time Arcade (page 144)

1. upside down exit sign; 2. monster arm reaching out of video game; 3. customer's hat floating; 4. no stool under customer on far left; 5. tail around leg of video-game player; 6. second stool from left is too tall; 7. second customer from right has no head; 8. section of the counter is missing; 9. third customer from left's head backwards; 10. far right customer has eyebrow but no eye; 11. spider hanging from ceiling; 12. no chain for one hanging light

Number Translation (page 144)

A	B	C
8	1	6
D	**E**	**F**
3	5	7
G	**H**	**J**
4	9	2

Proverb Chains (page 145)

1. He who hesitates is lost.
2. A bird in the hand is worth two in the bush.
3. When the cat's away, the mice will play.
4. Do unto others as you would have others do unto you.

Let's Get Cooking! (page 146)

There are 110 dots.

Animal Names (page 146)

1. hippopotamus; 2. hamster; 3. lion; 4. giraffe; 5. rabbit; 6. mountain goat; 7. elephant; 8. opossum; 9. moose; 10. rhinoceros

How Does Your Garden Grow? (page 147)

The flower below appears 7 times.

Sketchbook (page 148)

Equilateral Dismemberment (page 149)

Each figure contains 120 equilateral triangles.

Wise Wizard (page 149)

The wizard uses the dirt from the tunnel to make a pile high enough for him to climb up to the window and crawl out.

Cubic Crazy (page 150)

Figure D.

Stack the Deck (page 151)

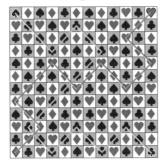

A Startling Word Puzzle (page 152)

Just as we said, the answer is STARTLING! The words you create from it may vary.

STARTLING − L = STARTING
STARTING − T = STARING
STARING − A = STRING
STRING − R = STING
STING − T = SING
SING − G = SIN
SIN − S = IN
IN − N = I

Shakespeare's Women (page 153)

Leftover letters spell:
LADY NORTHUMBERLAND

A Tangle of Triangles (page 154)

The missing number is 6. In each triangle, adding the numbers in the corners together, then adding the 2 numbers of that sum together, give you the middle number.

Tourist Attraction (page 155)

1. Dover; 2. islet; 3. singer; 4. nectar; 5. elbow; 6. Yemen; 7. wordy; 8. olive; 9. Rhine; 10. loiter; 11. decal. Tourist attraction: Disney World

Word Jigsaw (page 157)

Headline Howlers (page 157)

1. Kids make nutritious snacks. 2. Red tape holds up new bridges. 3. Astronaut takes blame for gas in spacecraft. 4. Plane too close to ground, crash probe told.

Answers

Rhyme Time (page 158)

1. own bone; 2. flan fan; 3. built silt; 4. freak leak; 5. swipe pipe; 6. light white; 7. snide guide; 8. bleak creek; 9. untold gold; 10. gruff enough; 11. metal kettle; 12. quaint paint; 13. explore more; 14. height fright; 15. extreme dream; 16. introspective detective; 17. imaginary dairy; 18. oodles of noodles; 19. discreet retreat; 20. college knowledge

Chip off the Old Block (page 159)

The correct piece is D.

Petalgrams (page 159)

officer, magnify, alfalfa, uniform, referee, leftist
Bonus word: formula

Similar Lines (page 160)

1. fit as a fiddle; 2. blind as a bat; 3. clean as a whistle; 4. light as a feather; 5. pretty as a picture; 6. slow as a tortoise; 7. stubborn as a mule

Diamond in the Rough (page 161)

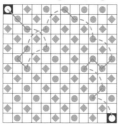

Eat Your Words (pages 162–163)

Take a Number! (page 164)

										43
2	3	6	4	5	6	2	9	1	9	47
3	1	8	7	6	1	2	2	3	8	41
4	6	5	4	3	7	4	8	1	9	51
2	4	5	7	8	5	6	4	3	1	45
1	2	9	3	5	6	7	8	9	1	51
7	4	3	2	2	1	4	5	5	2	35
8	9	8	1	1	4	2	8	5	9	55
6	2	1	7	6	5	2	4	2	8	43
9	5	6	7	8	4	1	3	1	3	47
2	4	3	9	8	7	6	5	4	4	52
44	40	54	51	52	46	36	56	34	54	32

Forget-Me-Not and Friends (pages 165–166)

MAGNOLIA, BUTTERCUP, JASMINE, DAFFODIL, DAISY, FORGET-ME-NOT, CARNATION, ALOE

Stargazer (page 167)

Group I: stars 2, 7, 11, 15
Group II: stars 3, 5, 12
Group III: stars 4, 9, 14
Group IV: stars 1, 13
Group V: stars 6, 10
Group VI: star 8

Hint for Letter Quilt, page 86

Prove bottommost cell of fourth column must contain A. Prove rightmost cell of fourth row must contain A.

Hint for Letter Quilt, page 118

Figure out which of 6 top-row cells contains B and which of 6 bottom-row cells contains C.

INDEX

Anagrams
Anagram Inventor, 142
Backyard Barbecue, 26
First Song, 31
Grab Bag, 57
M Is for Mystery, 125
Shall We Dance?, 34
Tourist Attraction, 155

Cryptograms
Animal Names, 146
Classic Lit, 116
Headline Howlers, 157
Last Laugh Department,
    100–101
Time Capsule, 20

Drawing Exercises
Mirror, Mirror, 24, 37, 88, 124,
    139, 156

Language Puzzles
Alternate Universe?, 62
Anagram Inventor, 142
Animal Farm, 53
Animal Names, 146
Back at You, 56
Backyard Barbecue, 26
Between the Lines, 44, 74–75
Born in 1875, 63
Bungle Gym, 62
But-Not Game, The, 36
City Sites, 59
Classic Lit, 116
Crazy Mixed-Up Letters, 40
Famous Address, 87
Famous Last Line, 95
Finding You, 12
Find the Booty!, 82
First Song, 31
Fitting Words, 30, 58, 70, 78,
    103, 117
Flying High, 19

Four Sisters, 112
Grab Bag, 57
Headline Howlers, 157
Hello, My Name Is Wrong, 16
Hidden Critters, 69
Inching Along, 43
It's a Song, 126
Jumbled Idiom, 20
Last Laugh Department,
    100–101
Let Freedom Ring, 91
Max and Mitch, 28
Merit Badge, 102
M Is for Mystery, 125
Missing Connections, 66
Motel Hideout, 76
Name Calling, 13, 21, 30
Petalgrams, 159
Proverb Chains, 145
Rhyme Time, 11, 23, 39, 55,
    72, 106, 137, 158
Scrambled Squares, 84
Shall We Dance?, 34
Similar Lines, 160
Startling Word Puzzle, A, 152
Take 30, 84
Tamagram, 59
Three for Two, 123
Time Capsule, 20
Tourist Attraction, 155
Vocal Vowels, 96
Wacky Wordy, 61, 126
Where Are the Animals?, 18
Wise Wizard, 149
Word Columns, 21, 71, 82, 99
Word Jigsaw, 17, 23, 48, 60,
    94, 97, 107, 127, 143, 157
Word Ladder(s), 14, 29, 35, 47,
    58, 87, 115

Logic Puzzles
Animal Names, 146
Circles and Numbers, 121

Classic Lit, 116
Coffee Break, 133
Count Down, 47
Count on This!, 14
Digital Sudoku, 70
Fair Freddy's Fondue Fete,
    114
Four Sisters, 112
Fun with Numbers, 95
Headline Howlers, 157
Last Laugh Department,
    100–101
Let's Make Some Music, 41
Letter Quilt, 86, 118
Logidoku, 90, 102, 107
Motel Hideout, 76
Number Challenge, 49
Number-Crossed, 109
Number Crossword, 71
Number Translation, 144
Odd-Even Logidoku, 135,
    143
Plus and Minuses, 121
Red, White, and Blue, 98
Roman Numerals Challenge,
    103
Sign of the Times, A, 78
Star Power, 35, 96, 120, 128,
    136
Sudoku, 12, 42, 63, 138
Sum Fun, 43
Take a Number!, 164
Tangle of Triangles, A, 154
Time Capsule, 20
Times Squared, 86, 114
Toys, 68
X × IV, 118

Math Puzzles
Circles and Numbers, 121
Coffee Break, 133
Count Down, 47

continued on page 192

Index

Math Puzzles
continued from page 191
Count on This!, 14
Fair Freddy's Fondue Fete, 114
Four-midable Maze, A, 122
Fun with Numbers, 95
Letters to Numbers, 52
Misleading Sequence, 66
Motel Hideout, 76
Multiples of Six Number Maze, 138
Number Challenge, 49
Number-Crossed, 109
Number Crossword, 71
Number Translation, 144
Plus and Minuses, 121
Roman Numerals Challenge, 103
Sign of the Times, A, 78
Sum Fun, 43
Take a Number!, 164
Times Squared, 86, 114
Toys, 68
X × IV, 118

Memory Puzzles
Forget-Me-Not and Friends (Parts I and II), 165-66
Sketchbook, 148
Sloop John B. and Co. (Parts I and II), 67–68

Mazes
Bit Askew, A, 36
Car Chase, 85
Diagonal Jump, 130
Diamond in the Rough, 161
Four-midable Maze, A, 122
Multiples of Six Number Maze, 138
Road Trip!, 134
Stack the Deck, 151

Observation and Perspective Puzzles
Around Five Cubes, 129
Chip off the Old Block, 159
Copycats, 52
Cube Fold, 92
Cubic Crazy, 150
Diagonal Jump, 130
Diagonal Switch, 77
Diamond in the Rough, 161
Don's Diner and Part-Time Arcade, 144
Equilateral Dismemberment, 149
Face the Blocks, 97
Fish Fantasy, 25
Flower Shop, 110
Gone Fishin', 13
How Does Your Garden Grow?, 147
Jigstars, 111
Layer by Layer, 29, 31
Let's Get Cooking!, 146
Match-Up Twins, 54
Overload of O's, 83
Planks Galore, 90
Quilt Quest, 16, 60, 94, 135
See Your Name in Print!, 38
Seven Slices, 22
Shoe Sale, 132

Sketchbook, 148
Stack the Deck, 151
Stargazer, 167
Swimming with the Cubes, 73
Tessellated Floor, 48
Ubiquity of U's, 45
Unbearable Jigsaw, 89
W-Cubed Rectangles, 119
What's for Dinner?, 79
X-Hibit of X's, 42

Sequencing
All Together Now, 83
Counting Up, 108
Good Book, The, 26
It's Old, 38
You Can't Have a Slice of This…, 115

Visual Logic Puzzles
ABCD, 91
Cast-a-word, 93, 99
Crisscross Puzzle, 113
Cross Count, 93, 133
Forget-Me-Not and Friends (Parts I and II), 165-66
Fruit Vendor's Cart, The, 27
Game On!, 22
Geometric Shapes, 17, 28, 108, 127, 131
Triple-Jointed, 50–51

Word Searches
All the Colours of the Rainbow, 80–81
At the Movies, 32–33
Bears Repeating, 61
Cross Earth, A, 140–41
Eat Your Words 162–63
Horsing Around, 64–65
How Will You Conduct Yourself?, 46
My Kind of Town, 104–5
Shakespeare's Women, 153
Thirsty?, 15